CONTENTS

CONSTRUCTION PLANS

APPENDICES

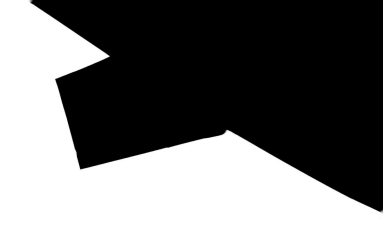

STUNT KITES

To Make and Fly

Text
   Servaas van der Horst en Nop Velthuizen
Photographs and Drawings
   Jan Pit

UITGEVERIJ THOTH

...ok is the English translation of a comp... ...tten and vastly extended version of ...unt Special' from the Dutch magazine *Vlieger* (*Kite*), as it appeared in april 1989.
The authors' acknowledgements are extended to the members of the stunt kiting team 'Crash' (Els Boelhouwer, Peter Ruinard, Michèle Velthuizen and Ed Wens) and to Guus van Dee, Frans van der Horst Sr., Tom van der Horst, Chris Kirkland, Arno van Leeuwen, Gerard van der Loo, Judy Neuger, Dominique Scholtes, Gerard Scholtes and C.M. de Vries for their indispensable cooperation.

The authors would especially like to thank 'J.R.K.' for voluntarily taking upon the difficult task of translating the manuscript into English.

Servaas van der Horst & Nop Velthuizen

ISBN 90 6868 052 8

Copyright © 1993
    Servaas van der Horst/Nop Velthuizen
    and THOTH Publishers, Bussum, the Netherlands
Photographs and Drawings
    Jan Pit
Cartoons
    Arno van Leeuwen
Photographs
    page 7 Flexifoil England Ltd
    page 11 Gerard van der Loo
    page 29 Robert Scheers
Graphics
    Eric van den Berg, Utrecht
Printing
    Haasbeek Printers Pte. Ltd., Alphen aan den Rijn

Distribution in the USA by What's Up
4500 Chagrin River Road, Chagrin Falls, Ohio 44022, USA
Tel. 216-247-4222 Fax 216-247-4444

Distribution outside the USA (Kite Shops) by
Vlieger Op bv, Weteringkade 5a, 2515 AK Den Haag, the Netherlands
Tel. 70-3858586 Fax 70-3838541

Distribution outside the USA (Bookshops) by
THOTH Publishers, Prins Hendriklaan 13, 1404 AS Bussum, the Netherlands
Tel. 2159-44144 Fax 2159-43266

INTRODUCTION

This is a book on the new outdoor sport for the nineties: stunt kite flying. A stunt kite is a maneuverable kite. By means of two or four control lines the stunt kite flyer can make his flying machine do everything he wants. Blustering over a deserted beach at over 200 km/h? No problem. Performing an aerial ballet to music in almost calm weather with a couple of friends? Can be done too. Stacking ten stunt kites and have yourself be dragged a dozen miles along the beach? No problem either. Almost anything is possible with the new style light-weight, but strongly built stunt kites that are accurately maneuverable. For all types of winds, from anything between the lightest breeze and a full storm, there is a stunt kite obeying your every wish, or whim for that matter.

This comprehensive book has been written for two categories of stunt kite flyers: for those that have bought a kite and now want to run the thing for all it is worth and for the stunt flyer who wants to build his own kites. So in the second part of this book you will find many detailed construction specifications for eleven different kite models, from very simple types to extremely complicated designs.

We also supply you with information on stunt kite history, control lines, knots, flying techniques, suitable flying grounds, constructions, sewing techniques, maneuvers and team flying.

To top it all, we present the stunt kite with which we broke the world speed record in the spring of 1991. The old record was established by a standard Flexifoil at 199 km/h, we flew an unofficial record of 228 km/h with a Speedfoil. So dig your feet in the sand and lean back, far back!

1 NEW-STYLE STUNT KITING

1. Paul E. Garber's Target Kite.

There have been stunt kites for centuries. In his famous book *Kites, an Historical Survey* (cf. Appendix 8) Clive Hart shows how the Chinese already made kites with multi-control lines. He did not make it quite clear whether stunting was a real feature of these Chinese kites. Hart makes mention of bird-type kites with wings that could be moved by separate lines. In the early 19th century the English schoolteacher George Pocock controlled his archtop kites with four lines, thus enabling his kites to pull a little cart, a so-called *char volant*, slantways against the wind. In World War II the American navy used Paul E. Garber's maneuverable kite as a mark for target practice. The five-foot high kite, suitably named *Target Kite*, showed the silhouette of a Japanese fighter plane so as to make the whole thing more lifelike. After it had been demonstrated to both the Army and the Navy authorities, the latter decided to try out 1,500 of these kites at first. The kites gave every satisfaction, so that a second order for

125,000 pieces was placed. In his book *Kites* Ron Moulton looks upon Garber's *Target Kite* as the prototype of all modern stunt kites.

As for our part the history of the new-style stunt kite starts with a different one, the *Peter Powell*. Powell, a boisterous Englishman, was the first to design an almost indestructible stunt kite. Its shape was hardly spectacular, a kind of Eddy type with two small tubes in the upper oblique sides. However, its construction and the application of the material were cleverly worked out. The stunter's sail was made of a heavy-quality polyethylene, whereas its frame consisted of aluminum tubing. Soon after that, the aluminum frame was replaced by a glass fibre frame, reinforcing the kite even more. The Powell stunter got a 25 meter long self-expanding tubular plastic tail. The Peter Powell's real breakthrough came in 1975. Ever since that period tens of thousands of Powells have been sold worldwide. To this very day the Powell belongs to the most popular stunt kites.

With the arrival in 1976 of the *Flexifoil* the stunt flying image changed radically. For the first time in history we had a kite looking fundamentally different from the well-known long-tailed Eddy type. The Flexifoil is a maneuverable wing, invented more or less by accident by two English industrial-design students. In the early seventies Ray Merry and Andrew Jones were supposed to create a work of art at some course, inspired by a certain word. These gentlemen chose the word *winding* and then tried to get all kinds of plastic bags up flying in the air.

Launching various objects into the air turned out to be easier than expected. Some time later the objects were given a wing profile - copied from glider models - and these climbed even better. Through a series of blunders, chance hits and clear examples of lucid thinking, our students managed to present in October 1976 a wing, maneuverable by two lines, thereby breaking all speed and tractive records.

The Flexifoil's secret is in the combination of the clever wing profile (cf. detailed construction drawing on page 77) and the tapered fibreglass nose rod holding the kite in a stretched position. Bridles or similar devices are not necessary; the model self-adjusts its wing position in relation to the wind, thanks to its clever profile. Even today, so many years later, the Flexifoil is still unbeatable in many respects. At stormy winds (8 Beaufort) for example, it is one of the few types we dare fly without fearing for its construction. And since this Flexifoil is so clever as to always seek the optimal angle of attack, it is theoretically the fastest stunt kite in the world. What's more, even in practice it is the fastest type. With a (modified) Flexifoil one can indeed break a speedkiting world record. So far we got stuck at 228 km/h.

For years now Flexifoils have been used as an alternative sail on sailing boats in races. A catamaran especially equipped for the purpose is fitted with a train of large Flexifoils (a so-called Jacob's Ladder, after the Scriptures story in which the patriarch Jacob dreams about an endless ladder reaching into heaven), thus obtaining much higher speeds than with a conventional sail. Conventional sails tend to make the boat capsize in proportion to the increasing wind-force, but Flexifoils only pull a boat out of and not into the water with increasing winds.

Flexifoils have their limits too. Many people are not too fond of their shape (they are often

2. Ray Merry launching a prototype of the Flexifoil. The kite was made of polyethylene and not sewn but sealed. The material of its spreader was wood, supported in the middle by a third line.

3. A stack of 15 Flexifoils (Jacob's Ladder) serving as a sail on a sailing-boat.

called 'flying mattresses'), whilst at little wind the Flexifoil is hardly an exciting kite, only to be forced into tight turns at great pains.

This is also a handicap with other flying wings of a more recent date. The strutless *Paraflex* of the German Wolfgang Schimmelpfennig, for example, needs a slightly stronger wind than the Flexifoil, but is just as fast while exceeding its pull.

Our own designs, *Sputniks 1 & 2*, are also completely folding. We found our inspiration from the wide paragliders, a kind of cross between a parachute and a delta wing, with which people have been throwing themselves from mountain sides in the posh French skiing resorts recently. This stunt wing too needs some wind to get going.

4. Team-Lights in formation. Uncomplicated even at minimal wind-force.

5. The 'William Tell trick' for solo flyers.

6. Can you beat this?! Team flying with four Cicadas.

That is why it is so exciting that in 1986 *stunt deltas* came in the picture. Some of them fly even at 1 Beaufort. They look great with their fine shapes and bright colors, developing a tremendous pull while accurately dirigible to every inch through the skies. Stunt deltas first flourished in that part of the United States where the sun always seems to shine: California. As their name suggests, these stunt kites are of a triangular (delta) shape, actually not really original. For the single-line deltas have existed ever since the mid-sixties. No, it is the application of the material and their construction that make these kites so new. Stunt deltas are made of the very best materials available at present. Even a Space Shuttle does not contain more modern material than a hi-tech stunt delta.

The frame of such a stunt kite consists of carbon and glassfibre tubing whilst the lightest conceivable spinnaker nylon is used. The control lines are practically free of stretch and weigh almost nothing. Combined with a good kite design and an ingenious bridle build-up, a type of kite is created that flies in an essentially different manner from those known so far. Some models can revolve on their axis so fast that your eyes can hardly follow the movement. With a stunt delta you can write all over the sky exactly the way you want it, with a stunt delta you are in *Total Control*.

Soon after the invention of the new-style stunt kite some new methods of stunt flying were developed. No doubt the most spectacular one being *team flying*. Some two to six flyers arrange themselves in a row, each one with the same model kite. One of them is appointed leader with the task to give various orders: he/she calls out the flying maneuvers. Provided these maneuvers blend into each other fairly well, you will have a complete aerial ballet, a magnificent sight.

Within a brief period several professional teams sprung up, training for hundreds of hours on the most perfect stunt shows. These fanatics often present their shows with musical accompaniment, taking care that their kites are moving to the rhythm of the music, whereas the very good ones among them even manage to make the musical emotions coincide exactly with the emotions expressed by certain flying maneuvers. When the music goes

8

crescendo, with drum-rolls for example, the kites will come speeding down, only to miss a fatal impact with the planet Earth by taking a fast turn-away, all to the loudspeakers' triumphant sound of trumpets.

Solo flying too is very attractive. The flyer will thread his control lines through a ground stake and stand right under his own stunt kite. Instead of annoying other people, you can thus 'fly yourself' a hole in your own head. High-virtuosity flyers are even capable of controlling two kites by themselves, *dual stunting*. One of the two lines of each kite is tied to the flyer's waist. The pilot holds the remaining two lines in his hands. Even *tri-stunting* is possible. Ron Reich from San Diego, California, controls two kites with his waist and his hands, then adds a third kite which he controls with his hips, a sight to make your head spin.

With the invention in 1988 of the *Speedwing*, new-style stunt flying has come within everybody's reach. The Germans Eric Heid, Thomas Erfurth and Harald Schlitzer developed a spineless kite, combining a simple construction with great speed, pull and maneuverability. In a few hours do-it-yourself, anybody can now have a kite doing a 175 km/h at 6 Beaufort. Moreover, this kite is capable of dragging a grown-up along the beach in spite of its small size of approx. 0.35 m^2. Quite amazing!

But things can run even wilder. Since 1988 we have the *Revolution*, a creation of the American Hadzicki brothers Dave, Jim and Joe. This kite is not controlled by two lines, but

7. Peter Lynn in his kite buggy, sliding through a curve.

8. The four-line Revolution stunter surpasses all expectations.

9. A train of Aces causing lots of fun at a Dutch flying site.

by four. This fact makes it possible to do a couple of things that other stunters cannot, such as flying backwards, spinning like a propeller, or coming to a sudden standstill in the middle of a deadly dive. On seeing it fly for the first time, most spectators usually cannot believe their eyes. This stunter surpasses all expectations.

In this book we did not supply the construction drawing of a Revolution. In its place, however, we presented the drawings for a four-line stunter, in the U.S. cleverly abbreviated as *quad*, very simple to build and doing everything a Revolution does.

The latest development in new-style stunt kiting is *buggy riding*. Peter Lynn from New Zealand improved upon this exciting sport, which is not altogether without danger. His source of propulsion is an extremely advanced sparless kite, called *Peel*, comparable to the Sputniks in this book (cf. page 78). Lynn's invention is shaped like the wing of the famous WW-II *Spitfire* fighter, i.e. elliptic. It is made in two sizes: 2.5 m^2 and 5 m^2. Normally the larger Peel is used; however, at near-gale wind-forces a switch is made to the smaller type.

The buggy is a three-wheeled cart that can be disassembled and is made of stainless steel. The pilot is seated beween the two back wheels and steers the buggy's front wheel with his feet. The pilot launches the Peel, gets onto his buggy and by clever maneuvering of the kite he can steer his buggy in almost all directions, as far as some 45° close to the wind. The buggy's ride is so smooth that high speeds can be effortlessly attained. Riding on a cross-wind course can result in the cart running at even higher speeds than the wind. Speeds up to some 90 km/h have been attained. (Don't forget your racing-helmet.)

For the nautical aficionado Peter Lynn has developed a trimaran that can also be disassembled. The central hull protrudes beyond the two outer hulls and can be steered with both feet. The procedure is similar to that of the buggy: launch the kite, get onto the trimaran and sail off. The highest speed so far has been 20 knots. Disassembling takes a few minutes only; when packed in a bag, it does not take up more space than a small surf-board. Now you'll get somewhere... literally.

2 THE FLYING SITE

An ideal flying site is sometimes hard to find, for you have to bear in mind two things: the wind and the safety of both the spectators and yourself.

Stunt kiting can be a dangerous activity. With strong winds the kites will reach very high speeds, exceeding 200 km/h. Hi-tech control lines are thin and sharp. A collision with a casual passer-by may have serious consequences. We have seen some awful injuries and burns. Therefore never fly right over the heads of promenaders, although it might perhaps be quite tempting to show them your kiting abilities by skimming ever so close along their naked necks. Under such circumstances a collision is almost unavoidable. Don't do it!

When launching the stunt kite it is a must to wait until everyone has left the place. During the first few feet of their flight these kites are practically unsteerable, producing the strangest antics. When about to lauch your kite you will notice that children especially like to stand as close as possible to the 'big and colorful thing'. Ask them to stand off a couple of yards; only then can you launch your kite safely.

Stunt flyers need a lot of space. Especially when ordinary one-line kites are also flown at that particular site, due consultations with your fellow aeronauts are definitely necessary. Never stand amidst others at crowded grounds, but try to split up the site in such a way that a collision becomes impossible. And, do maintain an unpretentious attitude towards the owners of ordinary kites. Their nylons are defenceless against your knife-sharp Kevlar lines, while giving way to your stunter is next to impossible. So leave them alone as much as possible.

Stunt kiting is not only dangerous to spectators; stunt flyers themselves have been known to fall victim to their own hobby. On the Ymuiden beach, near Amsterdam, a young stunt kite flyer met with a fatal accident in January 1992 while occupied in what is called *manlifting*. For this kind of *macho flying* the stunt kite is connected to a harness worn by the pilot. The harness in its turn is connected to a pole or any other heavy object on the ground by means of a line. When the kite goes up, the line will tighten itself and the flyer goes up too. The Dutch boy used a good harness and the right kite, he stood on the right place, i.e. an open beach with an on-shore wind, and he was an experienced flyer. Yet he was taken by surprise when the wind suddenly fell off, causing him to tumble down some 5 metres. He fell in such an unfortunate manner that he died in hospital eventually.

The year before, at the American East coast a quite experienced stunt kite flyer also crashed seriously while manlifting. The left side of his pelvis was shattered. He too employed the right material and had a lot of experience. Manlifting is an accident-prone activity. So, manlifting? Never!

The same applies to what is called *jumping*. With jumping the pilot hops over the beach like a kangaroo. This is caused by the flyer who, having so many square meters of kite on his line, not only shoots forwards but upwards as well. Hops of some 30 metres far and some 7 metres high have already been accomplished. It certainly looks very spectacular, the whole

beach crowd applauding for you, but in fact it's no more than stupid vanity. The kites may collapse, the wind may die, lines can break, or you might make a steering error. The result: your falling down from 7 metres high with a braking-chute which fails to open up. Moreover, the beatings you take each time you come down have proven to be particularly bad for your knees and ankles. Stop jumping!

Okay, so now you have decided to go stunt kiting the 'normal' way, wondering where the most suitable wind is to be found. The most obvious site is the beach, where the wind can blow uninterruptedly from sea or ocean. Stunt kites need an even, steady wind. You cannot just pull a stunt kite right across the tree tops, like you do with a one-line kite. You will soon find yourself at the edge of the field, while your kite flutters helplessly down to the ground. Built-up areas, industrial districts, mountains and woods, they all make stunt kiting practically impossible. A waste of time.

Do you live too far away from the beach? In that case look out for the sparse spots in the landscape where the wind can blow freely: on river banks, dikes, at lakesides, in open fields. Stand off from wind-disturbing obstacles. A good rule of thumb is that the wind is disturbed or *foul* over a stretch of twenty times the height of an obstacle. If the trees are 5 metres high you will have to stand off these trees at a distance of at least some hundred metres.

You also have to mind some other things. Stunt kiting by the side of a freeway is absolutely out of the question. You might distract a driver's attention, with fatal consequences. It is doubtful whether your third party insurer would pay for the damage caused. Do not fly your stunter near high-tension cables either. We know by experience that a small village can thus be cut off from power within a surprisingly short span of time!

3 THE CONTROL LINES

The control lines constitute the most underrated part of the stunt kite. Control lines can make or unmake a kite. If, for instance, you fly a very expensive carbon fibre racing-delta at 2 Beaufort with thick nylon lines of 135 kg breaking strength, you will have a very disappointing kiting day. There will be no way to get it moving, its lines hanging down heavily in the air, whilst the delta is only reacting very slowly to your maneuvering movements. The very same kite flown on twisted Spectra of 35 kg suddenly appears to be an accurately maneuverable, heavily pulling monster, forcing you to plant your heels firmly into the sand. So by choosing the right control lines you will have much more fun flying a stunt kite, hence the extensive information following below.

As a kite flyer you want a non-stretching, extremely smooth line, as thin as possible, and easy to knot.

Thin because weight, and especially wind-resistance have considerable influence on the kite. Radar-measuring a Flexifoil on Spectra lines of 90 kg showed a 15 percent slower flight than with Spectra lines of 65 kg breaking strength. In this case we are talking about a difference in diameter of not more than 0.2 mm (0.9 and 0.7 mm respectively)! Team flyers therefore prefer excessively thick lines at a fairly stiff breeze, so as to purposely lose speed. At minimal windspeeds thin lines are very important as the kite wants every bit of speed to gather sufficient lift.

Stretch should be minimal to establish direct contact with the kite. Especially with strong-pulling kites, such as the Speedwings, it is very tiring to make wide and fierce arm movements that are necessary to create almost square turns.

Tying knots. The comfort of easy-to-knot lines is evident, but unfortunately easy-to-knot lines do not exist. That is why you will find a separate paragraph on this art further down in this book (twining Dyneema/Spectra), in order to save as much strength in your lines as possible. **Smoothness** is a must, as you will usually control a stunt kite with at least two lines, which become entangled most of the time and must be capable of sliding over each other constantly. Smooth lines are even more important with team flying as your two lines sometimes have to compete with some ten other lines.

If you want to keep an eye on the said characteristics, you will have to stick to three criteria when buying your lines: breaking strength (10 - 1,000 kg), structure (twined, braided, with or without core, coarse or smooth) and material (nylon, Dacron, polypropylene, Kevlar, Spectra, and their combinations).

BREAKING STRENGTH

The choice of lines with the correct breaking strength is the first difficulty you will meet. You cannot assess the pull of the kite from its size without information as to its flight behaviour, such as its speed, or whether it was designed for strong or light winds.

Usually the breaking strength required for the kite is given; more often than not this factor is four or five times greater than the real pull of that particular kite.

1. This four-man wrap is only possible with Dyneema/Spectra.

STRUCTURE

The choice between the various structures is closely bound up with the choice of the material. In a twisted line the course of the individual fibres is much shorter than in a braided line. Hence you will have less stretch with a twisted line than with a braided one. In thin braided nylon lines - with a breaking strength of some 50 kg - stretch is unacceptably high.

The choice of a certain structure can also depend upon the surface of the line. The ribbed surface of twisted lines is clearly noticeable whenever these are rubbing over each other. A twisted line is also rather vulnerable: when one strand is damaged only two strands remain which soon will fray over a length of a couple of metres. A braided line, on the other hand, consists of six or more strands.

Braiding thin lines is an art and the manufacturer has a limited choice of fibre-bundles to compose his lines. Many thin bundles may produce a fine and smooth but expensive line; a limited number of thicker bundles often provides a somewhat coarser aspect. Moreover, the angle at which the braiding is done, as well as its pattern (e.g. one plain, two purl, etc.) are of great influence on breaking strength.

Dense braiding with many strands (twelve or more) produces a thicker line with the same strength, together with considerable non-elastic stretch. This means that during the first few flights the line will lengthen itself somewhat, because its fibres have space to settle. This is the reason why certain types of line, braided nylon in particular, have been pre-stretched by the manufacturer.

So, for the individual flyer it is hard to see whether a line has been properly braided or not. Choose a line which is as thin as possible for the given strength and with the smoothest possible surface.

MATERIAL

Dyneema/Spectra. The best base material for kite line fibres to date is High-Modulus-Polyethylene (HMP). The Dutch national 'chemistry pride' DSM has patented the process of aligning the super-long molecules within each fibre strand. This polyethylene fibre, which is being produced under the trademark of *Dyneema*, is ten times as strong as steel of equal weight and some forty percent stronger than aramide fibres (cf. Kevlar hereafter). This fibre's stretch is, at full load, 4 percent at the utmost. When applied in a braided line this figure may vary between 6 and 10 percent stretch in the line as a whole.

Next to Dyneema there is *Spectra* fibre, which is produced in the Unites States, and is of similar quality. Spectra is unbelievably smooth and is used by practically all team flyers all over the world. It has even been proven possible for 12 persons (i.e. 24 lines) to fly simultaneously and across each other without losing control.

The main disadvantage of Spectra/Dyneema is in its sensitivity for kite lines composed of other materials. If these lines are not made of polyethylene material, but ordinary nylon, sewing-cotton, Dacron or Kevlar, the super fibre will be beaten in nine cases out of ten. This fact is probably due to the low melting-point of the polyethylene fibre, roughly 150° C. Contact with other lines involves considerable frictional heat. Although 150° C. is not easily attained, the rapidly increasing heat causes a proportional decrease in tension strength.

Kevlar/Twaron stand for aramide fibres of comparable strength and stretch as Spectra/Dyneema at similar diameters. Kevlar is the trademark of Du Pont in the US, while Twaron originates from the Dutch chemical company of AKZO. For years Du Pont and AKZO have been charging each other with encroachment on patent rights for this aramide fibre. In the end an agreement was reached after each party realized that their lawyers cost more money than the profits from Kevlar/Twaron production.

Aramide fibres are affected by ultraviolet rays in sunlight, although no such problems have become known when put to use as kite lines. Ordinary daily wear is apparently a quicker process.

Lines made of these fibres show a stretch just as low as Spectra lines, but they give a much rougher feeling in normal use. Kevlar lines easily cut through someone else's lines, which seems to be an advantage over Spectra. But this is only temporary. When flying, these lines also fray themselves, which turns them even coarser. Moreover, a Kevlar pilot clearly does not make many friends on his flying terrain.

Dacron is a brandname for polyester. Both twisted and braided, Dacron constitute the best control lines for the low-budget kite flyer. Dacron is sufficiently smooth. As far as stretch is concerned, the material can be evaluated somewhere between nylon and Spectra, but its thickness is comparable to nylon lines.

The important question remains unsolved; why is this type of line unfit for team flying? It is smooth, and nicely braided, but in the very first wrap - even if it is only a dual team - the lines will break.

Skybond is something special. This line consists of a Kevlar core with a Dacron coating, protecting the Kevlar, so that the line is somewhat safer to fly with on crowded sites. It can be satisfactorily knotted, though you may count on some 30 percent loss in tension strength. This line has the lowest stretch of all kite lines, because the Kevlar fibres in its core have hardly been twisted, hence run straight through. But this line also has its disadvantages. It is a relatively heavy and thick line, therefore unfit for low wind-forces. Because of their extremely low stretch, the fibres are more often overloaded in gusts, causing a phenomenon comparable to metal fatigue. The line will suddenly break below the breaking point given.

This has nothing to do with the phenomenon of the Kevlar core protruding through the coating after some time. According to the manufacturer this is quite normal; under load the core will return to its original position.

Nylon line is best known for one-line kites. It fits this purpose particularly well, because it is cheap, reasonably strong and hardly vulnerable. Nylon is unsuitable for stunt kiting, its stretch being capable of mounting to far over 50 percent on maximum loads. Even pre-stretched nylon may still stretch considerably. When using thicker lines, say from 135 kg breaking strenght onwards, part of the objections to the use of nylon is disposed of. For those who love the big jobs, for example, long trains of Flexifoils, nylon will remain an acceptable and affordable alternative. Due to its considerable stretch, nylon will protect itself from material fatigue as described with the Skybond line.

Polypropylene. The usually rather coarse polypropylene fibre is altogether out of the picture as a kite line. It is of low density, hence very thick lines with relatively little tension strength. It makes for an attractive bridle line, because it has good knotting-strength due to its thickness. And it comes in nice colors as well.

2. You won't make many friends on your flying site with Kevlar lines.

LENGTH OF THE CONTROL LINES

The standard length of control lines is 45 metres, which is a lot less than the 60 metres in use for stunting until a short time ago. But even those 45 metres are still rather long. 35 metres would give the kite even more fierceness, particularly so when the cheaper, stretching lines are used. It has the advantage of taking up less space. The beaches are getting more and more crowded! The shorter your lines, the less wind you need to get your kite going. The shorter lines have less air drag, they weigh less and the kite will react in a more accute way to steering commands. It is of course of great importance to see to it that both lines are of equal length, or you would have to keep one hand closer to your body in order to make the kite fly straight on. Bear in mind that new lines will produce unequal stretch during the first few flying hours. It is not unusual having to adjust the lengths three or four times, and if, next time, there is a strong wind blowing, another adjustment will be necessary!

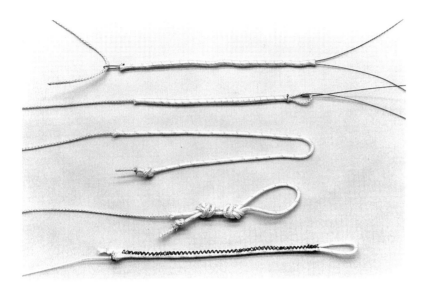

3. The control line is pulled through the sleeve by means of a thin doubled-up piano wire. Then a double overhand loop is made, or sewn in a zigzag fashion.

4. Knots, from left to right: half-hitch, overhand loop, larks head, larks head with extra loop, bowline knot, slip knot and blood knot.

TYING KNOTS IN LINES

We must distinguish right away between the tying of knots in control lines and knots in lines that are attached to the kite, such as bridle lines and tension lines. But first, control lines:

Tying knots in the new hi-tech lines is a matter of great care. A wrong knot in Spectra, for example, will reduce the space fibre to a mere twine; any jerk of the kite will break the line. Tests by the Belgian kiting magazine *La Nouveau Cervoliste Belge* have shown that the strongest fastening consists of a polyester sleeve round the end of the control line, not knotted, but sewn zigzag. Our own tests showed that at least 90 percent of the tension strength is preserved when the sleeve is sewn zigzag over 10 cm. It will be necessary, however, to start zigzagging on the loop-side, and from there sew towards the end of the sleeve. Having arrived there, you will turn round without cutting the thread while zigzagging back towards the loop.

With a knotted sleeve you will lose at least 15 percent of the tension strength. The line will stand it, but the knot is the weakest point, breaking time and again. For one practical reason we still prefer a knot at the end instead of the zigzag stitching. When a kite is pulling so hard that its pull is approaching the breaking point of the line, we'd rather have the line break at the knot than somewhere halfway. So you will lose a couple of inches of your expensive line instead of the whole reel. The knot is taking the role of a kind of fracture-plate, while the fracture point is under your control. Yet another advantage of knots is that you can apply changes in the lengths of your control lines while on the kiting site. Un-knot, shorten the longest line somewhat by pushing up the sleeve a little, and re-knot it (cf. the instructions below).

In order to make a protective sleeve you need some thick braided line of approx. 30 cm length. Remove the core (a fluffy strand of threads) from the line with your nails. Pull the control line through the sleeve by means of a thin doubled-up piano wire. Tie an ordinary overhand knot (cf. below) at the end. Use it once to fly your kite. The lines will no doubt stretch unequally. Shorten the longest line, check once again if both lines are of equal lengths now. If so, tie a second overhand knot in the loop, so as to prevent the control line from slipping inside the sleeve.

When you prefer to fasten the loops with zigzag stitching (e.g. because you correctly think that flying your kite with thinner lines will turn it into a faster kite), you have to construct

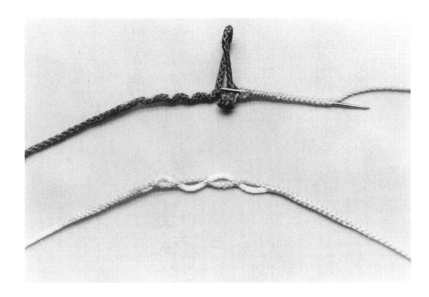

5. Broken Spectra/Dyneema can only be braided.

something at the grips-side, which will enable you to adjust the lengths of your lines. It is easy enough in the case of a Skyclaw (cf. below and nr. 4 Appendix): the V-line fastening the handle to the control line can be adjusted to the proper length right then and there.

   After a few months of kiting the lines will show wear on the spots where they cross each other when spinning the kite. Therefore, interchange the lines after some time: kite-side will become steering-side and the other way round. This way you can spread wear more evenly and enjoy the use of your lines for a longer period of time.

When tying knots in bridle lines you can work with less care, for these lines are much stronger than actually necessary. Here follows a list of the most widely used knots and their applications. From the pictures you can see how to tie them.

Half-hitch. The standard knot. At the ends of lines, to prevent them from fraying or slipping.

Overhand knot. Just a half-hitch in a doubled-over line. This knot is used for practically all loops in bridles. It is also the standard knot for making the end-loops of sleeved control lines.

Larks Head. Also called the circular knot or trimming knot. The knot to place rings or clips in a bridle that still wants easy trimming. With an extra loop around the ring you can fix the larks head firmly.

Bowline knot. The knot for loops that need quick undoing. The length of the loop with a bowline knot is not easy to adjust.

Slip knot. With this knot any adjustment is quite easy. After slipping the loose end through the half-hitch, you can adjust the loop to a millimetre. Then you keep the knot fixed on its place by tying a second half-hitch behind the first one.

Blood knot. The only knot permitting repair of a broken control line. Spectra cannot be repaired in this way, the material being too smooth, so that the knot will come undone within a few seconds.

BRAIDING SPECTRA

There is but one solution for broken Spectra: braiding. Use a blunt darning needle (a sharp point would damage the fibres) to braid one of the ends three times through the other line, starting at 5 cm from the rupture-point. With the darning-needle work the end away into the core of the line. Repeat the procedure with the other end; pull through three times and work away the loose end. This method is even stronger than a sleeve-and-knot, providing an entirely smooth connection.

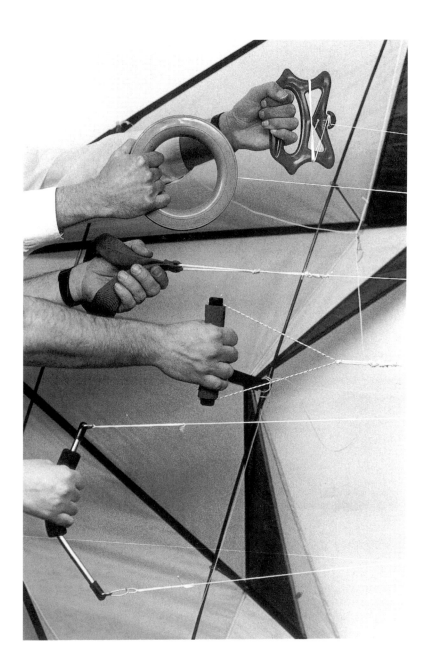

6. *Controlling gear. From top to bottom: Peter Powell grip, spool, padded strap, Skyclaw, Revolution-handle.*

GRIPS, CONTROL BARS AND PADDED STRAPS

In order to keep up stunt kiting for a while, the controlling gear in your hands must give a comfortable feeling. You can choose between grips, padded straps and control bars.

GRIPS

Nowadays grips are mostly used. They are certainly essential to team flyers. During team flying the members of the group are standing rather close to one another. Therefore it is necessary for the flyers not to poke at each other with the sharp ends of control bars.

The most beautiful grip is made by the American manufacturer Shanti, sold under the brandname of Skyclaw. It consists of two short sticks, covered with neoprene in two different colours. Neoprene is a kind of synthetical sponge, always feeling soft and warm. After flying the grips can be stored on a kind of small fork, enabling the lines to be rolled up without tangling them. A similar grip can easily be made the do-it-yourself way. You will find the construction drawing in the Nr.4 Appendix.

Next to the Skyclaw, the reinforced Peter Powell grips appear to meet the requirements. Do-it-yourself construction (with thick plywood) is hardly worth the effort, because the cost of material runs just as high. A clever feature of the Peter Powell grip is the small hook at its front, allowing for a quite simple way of trimming the control lines to the correct lengths, even in flight. It is also possible to have part of the lines remain on the grips, in the case of lack of space on the kiting site, for example.

7. A harness takes over part of the pull.

CONTROL BARS

Control bars take up a lot of space and are unfit for team flying. However, they do have certain advantages.

For instance, you can attach the bar at the middle to a harness around the hips; the kite will be pulling at your trunk, not at your arms. Very convenient for heavy work in a gale. Those of you who love the real big job - say, thirty Flexifoils in a train - had better make a control bar which is supported in the middle, for otherwise you may run the risk of breaking the bar.

PADDED STRAPS

There are two types of straps: one is made from strong band, whereas a lined type looks like a fat rounded sausage. These straps can be hooked behind the wrists or the elbows.

HARNESS

Not only control bars can be combined with a harness. Also grips and padded straps can be easily connected to a harness. The harness comprises a wide, adjustable band around the hips and two narrow bands around the legs (resembles a diaper). Two adjustable strips run from the wide band to the handles or padded straps, linked up with a snap-hook. While steering with bent arms, the full pull will affect your upper body. When tired, and slackening the arms somewhat, the strips will tighten and your hips will take over a great deal of the arms' work.

Warning! There is a danger in the use of harnesses: if the pilot loses his/her balance, he/she will be dragged along uncontrollably. Therefore, it is absolutely necessary to incorporate some form of quick-release mechanism in your harness. But remember, even then, this kind of 'power-kiting' is not 100 percent safe.

FINGER GRIPS

Finger grips for very exact maneuvering with little wind. These are in fact just small, light-weight straps.

BOBBINS

Finally there are round, plastic bobbins (reels). They are reasonably comfortable to the feel. Changing the length of the line is simplicity itself: just let the bobbin make one turn in your hand.

4 BRIDLE ADJUSTMENT

bridle clips upward, the kite is bridled 'high'

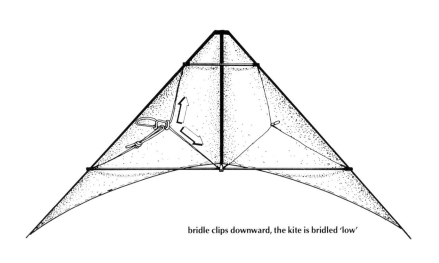

bridle clips downward, the kite is bridled 'low'

1. Bridle adjustment of stunt deltas.

2. A wrongly adjusted kite drops to the ground.

Suppose your first home-made stunt delta is ready. Or, you have just come back from the kite shop where you bought a magnificent specimen. Now only one thing remains to be done before the kite can be launched into the air: adjusting its bridle. In this chapter we will deal with those aspects of adjustment that are applicable to all types of stunt deltas. You will explicitly find any variances in the construction plan of each kite.

With a stunt kite, a bridle is responsible for two things: it determines the angle at which the wind will blow into the sail, and it enables controlling the kite. The bridle should be adjusted in such a manner that the kite will fly fast, at the same time maneuver well and pull hard. This is easier said than done. Here are some hints for you.

Make a bridle in accordance with the measures given in the construction plan. Wait for the right wind for your kite, go to a suitable kiting site and launch your delta. Make a short flight and remember accurately what the kite does. Now carry out some experiments with the bridling, making use of the following knowledge. When you shove the bridling clips downwards, away from the nose i.e., the kite's maneuverability will improve; its speed will increase

and therefore it will pull harder. When you move the clips upwards, i.e. towards the nose, the kite will maneuver worse, fly slower, hence develop a weaker pull.

From the above you might gather that it is only a matter of fastening the clips low enough on the bridle to get yourself automatically a super-fast kite. Unfortunately, things are not that easy. In the first place, a kite bridled too low will simply not fly at all. The thing will hop up some four inches or so, only to reverse and sag back onto the ground immediately. Secondly, it has been proven possible - especially in strong winds - to bridle your kite too low and still get it to fly. The kite, however, will be too sensitive to controlling commands and its speed will be exceptionally low. The kite will drag heavily and nervously. If such is the case, you have gone too far in shoving the bridling clips downwards.

It all boils down to flying your kite for the first time with the bridle in the position advised in our construction plans or as pre-set by the manufacturer of your kite. Now shove the clips down two millimetres at a time until the kite will not fly any longer, or is getting hyper-sensitive. Back up one millimetre and you have arrived at the ideal position.

3. A high-set bridle.

4. And a low-set bridle.

Experience has shown that a well-adjusted stunt delta is definitely hard to launch. During the first few metres it tends to fly sideways, tumbling powerlessly through the air, only to suddenly find its way while shooting off. So, don't panic when the launching is a somewhat difficult affair, it's all part of the game. Generally speaking, once a bridle is properly adjusted, you do not have to adapt it any more for another wind-force. Only when there is very little wind should you shove the clips a few millimetres upwards so as to be able to launch the kite at all. However, flying in this condition will turn out to be quite boring. When there is too much wind for your kite, if you insist on flying it, you can purposely put the clips too high. This will reduce the kite's pull and make it survive the gale.

When a kite does not steer evenly to the left, or to the right - e.g. it turns easier to the left than to the right - it is high time to check the control lines. If these appear to be of equal lengths, the symptom is due to an asymmetrical bridle. The bridle point is lower at that side where the kite makes its shortest turns, than at the other side. Shove the low clip somewhat upwards, or the high one a bit downwards.

5 FLYING YOUR STUNT KITE

1. Simply pull your left hand: the kite will turn left.

2. Skiing behind a train of Standard-200's across the sand drift: just hang on in a relaxed manner.

BEGINNERS

Stunt kiting starts off with the launching. Sometimes this is pretty difficult. The bridles of the stunt deltas are adjusted so low that the kites are having trouble getting started. So take along a mate to the flying terrain - certainly in the beginner's stages - who can help you with the launching. Wait for a day with a constant, moderate wind, say 3 to 4 Beaufort. Try to find the best terrain in the neighborhood. Roll out the control lines, remove any twists in the lines, and attach the lines to the kite. Make sure the lines will not get hooked behind any obstacle. The lefthand side of the kite has to be connected to the pilot's left hand. Wait until any passers-by have left; have your mate throw up the stunt kite into the air at a fair speed, the faster the better. Take good care not to do anything at all yourself!

The error usually made at this stage is to start jerking wildly at the control lines immediately after launching. A quite understandable reaction, but in doing so, you will pull the wind out of

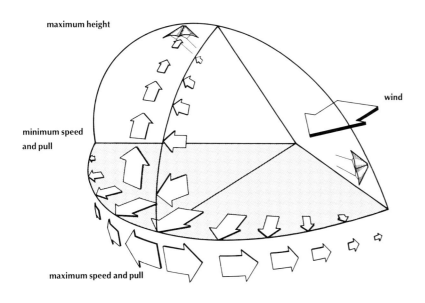

maximum height

minimum speed
and pull

wind

maximum speed and pull

3. Flying window. Decreasing pull at the top and the sides.

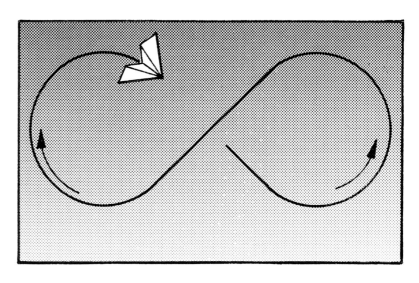

4.1 Infinity.

the kite's sail, and the kite will flutter helplessly back to the ground. No, you should give it a fair chance to get started. Just watch! Now the stunter suddenly dashes off, the fibre spars bending, the pull increasing all of a sudden and your sweat starts running along your spine. How to allay the growing panic? How can you ever get this screaming monster back on earth whole and safe?

Our advice: don't panic! The basic philosophy of stunt kiting happens to be extremely simple. If you pull the left control line, the kite will turn left. Pulling the right control line will make it steer to the right. Even the most intricate flying-pattern is nothing but a combination of these two movements. If you pull the left-hand line a bit longer, the kite will complete a full circle in the air, the lines getting twisted one turn. Nothing wrong with that, just pull the right-hand line. The kite will circle the other way, resulting in the lines undoing their temporarily twisted condition. Controlling a stunt kite is done the way you steer a bicycle: you move your hands away from and towards your body. A frequently made error is to steer a kite as you do a car: moving your hands upwards and down in a circular manner. This is not at all efficient. A stunt kite reacts on differences in length of the control lines.

You particularly control a stunt kite by very slight movements only. Modern control lines produce so little stretch that any slight shaking of your hand is reflected by your kite. There-fore hold your hands close to each other, arms slightly bent, your elbows beside your body. If

the pull is increasing, hang on backwards, your body in a stretched but relaxed stance. Avoid the well-known squatting posture, which no one can hold out for a long time.

You will soon discover that the kite in flight will not pull equally strong everywhere. When you send the kite far against the wind, or when you fly it right over your head, the pull will immediately fall off. When your hands can hold it no longer, park the kite there for a while. Speed and pull are at their height at that spot where the wind blows right onto the kite, in sailing-terms: downwind.

After, say, some thirty minutes your panic will abate and make place for a feeling of 'all systems go'. But now there is an imminent danger of recklessness, which we will have to deal with. Start flying some horizontal-eight patterns, called *infinities*, the direction of the turns pointing upwards. Then have the kite fly right over your head and try doing the *powerdive*: crash down to earth as fast as possible, only to deflect from this course at one metre or so above the ground. Everything still whole and sound? Good! Now make a landing. This is done by steering the kite left or right against the wind and then to the ground. The very moment it touches the ground, take one step forward. Finally, launching without assistance. Place the kite against a pole or stake, its nose slightly leaning backwards. Grab the handles and give them a controlled jerk, while taking a few steps backwards. This should do.

If you master all this, you are no longer a beginner.

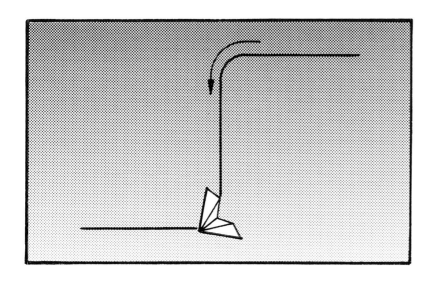

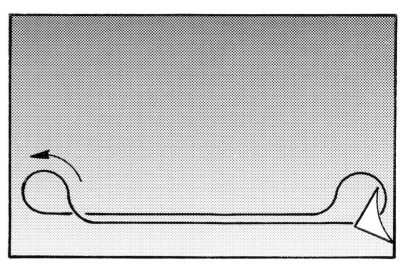

4.2 Powerdive.

4.4 Groundsweeps.

4.3 Gaining height in low winds.

4.5 Stepping down.

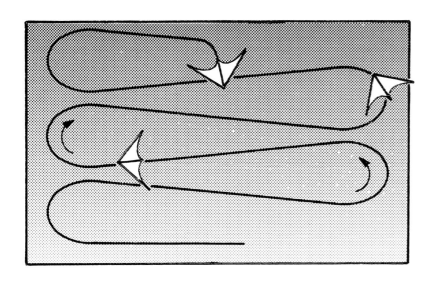

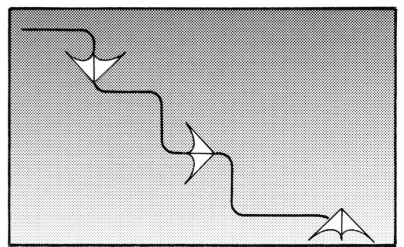

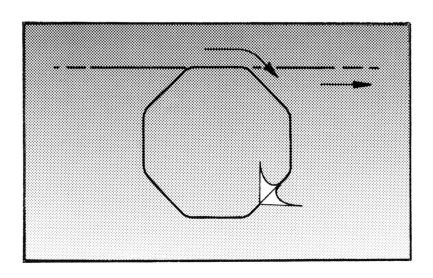

4.6 Octagon. Make sure your turns are 45°. Step forwards during the downward path of the pattern.

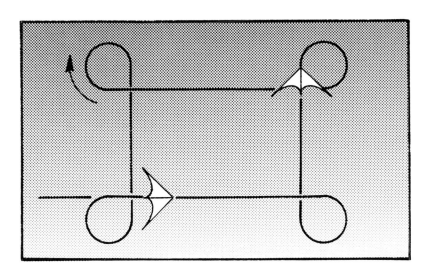

4.7 Clover-rectangles. Mind the timing in this pattern. Make sure the loops are exactly 270°. Keep the loops as small as possible, ending up on the same height as where you started.

ADVANCED FLYERS

With little wind good kite stunting will become harder. The most important thing, in any case, is to keep the kite moving by flying infinities. Don't go too far left or right into the wind. The decreasing tension in the lines will make you feel just how far you can go. Take care to maintain sufficient speed for an upward turn, while trying - as if you are climbing a ladder - to gain height. These very turns make you gain that necessary height. During the horizontal, or if necessary slightly descending paths, the kite will pick up sufficient speed for the next upward turn. With little wind downward turns will usually produce a mess-up, because you are then throwing your kite out of the wind, causing it to flutter down.

Flying the straightest possible lines is achieved by firmly holding on to a course once taken. Trying to make corrections is fundamentally wrong. For a fine straight flight turn the upper part of your body in accordance with the kite, keeping your arms stretched. You will preferably start the straight line by making a downward turn. The kite will immediately be at near-ground level, drawing a flawless straight line to the other side and popping up slightly at the end of its path; on taking a short-cut turn, it is back again on its straight return path: *groundsweeps*.

For a square turn all the kite needs is a steering pulse, a slight but fierce tug at one of its lines. Not all models can stand such a sudden tug and eventually will stall for a moment, in the worst case followed by a flight towards the ground. The remedy sometimes consists of giving it more line momentarily, instead of giving it a jerk. A kind of boxing jab. Definitely tiring.

You can land the stunt deltas in such a way that they will stand by, ready for the next flight. To do this you should fly the kite away to one side as far as possible. Just before it touches the ground, you steer its nose upwards, at the same time taking a few steps in the direction of the kite.

The problem with landing against the wind is that, sometimes, it is a hard job to launch it again from its landing-place, because of the wind blowing at an unfavorable angle into the sail. Advanced flyers, therefore, land their kites downwind, where the wind blows on the kite at a right angle and where the kite has its highest speed. For this type of landing, steer from one of the upper corners slantingly down towards the ground. With the kite rising just above the ground, you start walking forwards. The kite's speed suddenly decreases. While still walking you steer the kite upwards. The moment the kite is pointing its nose straight up, you take another three fast steps. The kite drops dead, landing neatly on its wing spars, ready for the next launching. This trick only works with little wind; with a stronger wind blowing, the kite will not drop dead but keeps on flying.

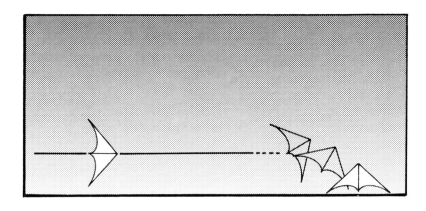

5. While landing, the kite is put on the ground against the wind.

HIGHLY ADVANCED FLYERS

A real ace of course does not move a single foot while landing his kite. Therefore: steer heading down at a blasting speed, then, at some 10 cm above the ground pull the kite in a radical spin which will cause it to stall immediately. Now just briefly stretch your arms, land... and the admiring glances will be yours.

6. This Revolution is hanging upside-down, in a stationary position.

FOUR-LINE CONTROL

Steering a four-line stunter is a basically different thing. The kite will not react to your hands just moving about. No, in principle you should keep your hands beside each other, at the same height. Steering is accomplished by sudden movements of your wrists, as if you are collecting money while jingling a collection-box for a street musician. When, for instance, you pull the lower part of the righthand grip towards yourself, the kite's righthand side will twist (i.e. turn round the central cross-strut) in relation to its lefthand side, which will cause the kite to spin to the right at lightning speed. When you move the lower parts of both grips towards yourself simultaneously, the kite will lose height backwards; when you move the grips' upper parts towards yourself, it will gain height. The problem with both the Revolution and our Kwat is that, during gaining and losing height, the kite needs corrections constantly: it easily deviates from its course. In the beginning you will automatically make these steering corrections as if you are flying a normal dual-line stunter, by pulling the left or the right line. Watch out, you are messing things up now. Should the kite run wild, there is no stopping it

7. Four-line control in four steps:
1. straight up
2. steady on the same spot
3. spin over the left side
4. put in reverse.

anymore. Don't worry, its construction can stand it, but do take a few steps forwards as your Kwat hits the ground.

At first, limit yourself to climbing and descending in a straight line. Once you have become used to this new feeling, try steering the kite into a spin. After a while you will notice that, after all, with some maneuvers it appears necessary to mutually move your hands a little as in the case of a two-line stunter. That is done, for instance, when you want to fly the kite transversely, i.e. steering it with the cross-strut parallel to the horizon from left to right. As soon as you master the combination of wrist-movements and differences in arm lengths, you can, in principle, fly upside-down, in reverse and even on its tip. Stuff for the highly advanced flyers.

A tip for owners of a Revolution: it has been proved in practice that it is quite possible to replace the original, relatively heavy Revolution frame by a 6-millimetre carbon frame (nowadays the Revolution is also available with an ultra-light spar set). Even with very little wind (2 Beaufort) the kite will gain height easily. But as soon as wind force is increasing, you will have to re-install the original frame!

6 TEAM FLYING

We mentioned it already in chapter 1: team flying is the most spectacular form of stunt kiting. Two to six flyers team up beside one another to go 'writing all over the sky' in a complicated manner without the lines getting seriously knotted (if performed properly). Advanced teams even do this to music, turning the whole performance into a real aerial ballet. In the United States a complete team flying circuit has sprung up, with sometimes big prize money, sponsors, judges and the inevitable bickerings. There are two disciplines: *Team Ballet* (to music) and *Team Precision*. In the precision competitions a number of obligatory patterns must be flown, followed by a free routine, i.e. a number of flight patterns blending into each other during a maximum of five minutes, in which the team can show its most complicated tricks. The more risky, the higher the score. The chances of eventually falling into errors of course grow proportionally.

Team flying is difficult, it takes a lot of time and money, but it is extremely exciting. In the following part we give you all information so as to enable you and your kiting friends to grow into a competitive stunt flying team.

THE KITES

In principle you can perform an aerial ballet with every type of kite, but sooner or later you will start making high demands upon the kites. After all, team flying is a hobby requiring lots of time, which makes it a nuisance when the kites themselves are the limiting factor. When you live in an area with freakish wind-forces, you will, as a team, first have to decide on the choice of just flying with one type for all wind forces, or on investing at once in two or three types fit for optimum performances in a variety of winds.

We would vote for the latter choice, thus avoiding compromises. Moreover, when used intensively the kites will have a tough time. Collisions in mid-air, dragging along the ground and scraping along the control lines, as well as many flying hours generate a lot of wear and tear. A strong wind model can cope very well with a gale, a light wind kite would be worn out in less than no time in that case, but will offer years of service with correct use. Besides, the diversity of the various models will turn your kiting into an ever so interesting activity.

It is certainly not true that only speedy, fast-pulling models are fit for team flying. On the contrary, team flyers have had the best of experiences with models moving at a relatively slow pace, and with little pull, through the air. You will then be in a better position to keep good control on the kites, there will be more time for decisions, at the same time you can keep up your efforts for a longer stretch of time.

THE CONTROL LINES

We can be brief with respect to the materials fit for team flying: these have to be Dyneema fibre or Spectra fibre. Braided Shanti Spectra and Spiderline Spectra are leading brands. Cheaper alternatives are braided Dyneema and twisted Spectra, which are quite satisfactory for beginning small teams flying not too complicated patterns without many twists in the lines.

1. Uppermost concentration in the stunt flying team of the Dike Hoppers.

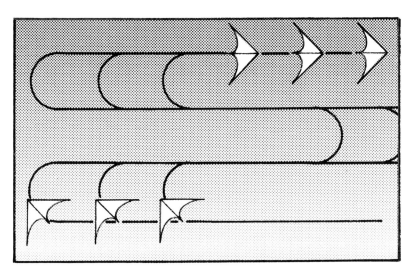

2. Relative length of lines, 1 metre shorter each.

3. 180° turn. After each turn the foremost kite becomes the hindmost one, and the other way round.

The most popular tension strength is 65 kg; 90 kg is second best for stronger flyers. The 45 kg type serves the very lightest winds, lines of 135 kg come in handy for very strong winds because both the weight and the air-drag of the lines will slow down the kites a bit. Don't forget that the team flyer does not like a flashingly fast kite at all!

The standard length of 45 metres is very useful for all types of team flying. But there are alternatives: 45 kg lines cut in halves of 22.5 metres for fierce duets in light winds, or 90 kg breaking-strength lines of 60 metres length for an extensive aerial ballet with big Flexifoils.

TEAM ADJUSTMENT

If the whole team flies with control lines of similar lengths, the followers will suffer continuously from foul wind, because they fly in the slipstream of their leaders. The easiest solution is to have the followers fly, stepwise, with lines one metre shorter each. For any beginning stunt team this is definitely the best method.

As the flying patterns get more complicated, you will notice, being the number two pilot, that you are not only following the number one flyer, but you will sometimes be following the numbers three and four, thus hanging even more in the slipstream because of the staged lines. The solution for this problem is to be found in footwork: walk backwards to get out of the slipstream. But don't count on having time - while busy team flying - to think about that solution consciously. That may be the case one season later. Staged-length control lines also have the advantage that the kites will not be able to collide with each other, preventing a lot of tedious repair work.

One source of damage to the lines must be blamed on the kites themselves. A frontal collision between a kite from the left and flying lines coming from the right can result in melted lines. This risk can be considerably reduced by applying a nylon jacket to the contact-area, i.e. the last few metres of control line. It is easier, however, to finish the last few metres in Kevlar or Skybond line. This also applies to the kite's bridling lines: do not hesitate to replace them by a strong aramide fibre.

TEAM ACCESSORIES

GROUND STAKE

One or more ground stakes are a must rather than an accessory. The most handy type is a big and strong stake in the ground, to which all kites can be tied simultaneously. Such a land anchor is used to compare and adjust the respective line lengths, to arrange the kites for a start without any outside assistance, as a 'parking place' during a coffee break, etc. For soft soils use the super-size corkscrew known as a dog-stake; for hard types of soils, use a tent-peg or an old screwdriver. Because these objects get lost regularly (people forget to pull them out of the ground at the end of the day, high tide comes in or someone mistakes it for his own groundstake), we advise you to tie a fluorescent ribbon to it.

SPARES

It would not be the first time that the left and right grip has been swapped before the first launch, causing the kite to plunge with a wide curve and under full wind pressure into the ground. Bang! a broken spine, or even worse. So take care to have a sufficient number of spare struts with you. Even a complete spare kite is no luxury for a team.

WEATHER-VANE

Especially on summer days with lots of thermals (updraughts) you will have to deal with constantly changing wind directions. In order to determine the centre-point, a weather-vane or a stationary kite can be very useful.

TAPE RECORDER

Each self-respecting stunt team will compose a routine (cf. stage 4, below). After having developed a routine, the next step will be its combination with music. There are different possibilities: one is a great big ghetto-blaster, so that the whole team can share the feel of the music. In that case the leader of the team has to shout down the tumult, while the promenaders on the beach are obliged to 'enjoy' the din too. Another possibility is to choose a 'walkman' for the leader only, but then the rest of your team will miss the charms of such an aerial ballet.

5. It looks ridiculous, but it works! A stunt kiting team with practice sticks.

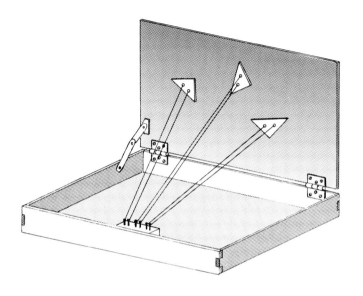

6. With the team simulator you can try out complicated flying patterns.

PRACTICE-STICKS

It does look rather absurd, but a stunt team of character can stand being laughed at occasionally. With cardboard team-kites made to a scale of 1 : 50 and nailed on top of short rods of some 75 cm length, it is quite easy to simulate your routine and, especially, new flying-patterns. It will prevent a few collisions and a lot of bungling in the air. Moreover, you can 'fly' in slow-motion which gives you lots of time to direct each team member to his or her exact place 'in the air'. The tiny kites are to a scale of 1 : 50 so as to maintain the same proportions as in reality: they give you the same optical impression as far as size is concerned, so their *spacing* (see below) and room occupied within the flying-window are also to scale.

SIMULATOR

What cannot be accomplished with practice-sticks, is the simulation of the control lines winding and twisting around each other. This might surprise you in an unpleasant way when thinking out new patterns: what looks very nice on paper, often appears to produce great big knots in reality. To discover these (im)possibilities you can use a small box with miniature-size kites stuck to its strong thin back wall by means of small magnets. Two super-thin elastic bands will connect each little kite to two nails (the grips or handles). With this team simulator you can try out the most fantastic 'wicker-works', which - believe it or not - can still be disentangled in the end.

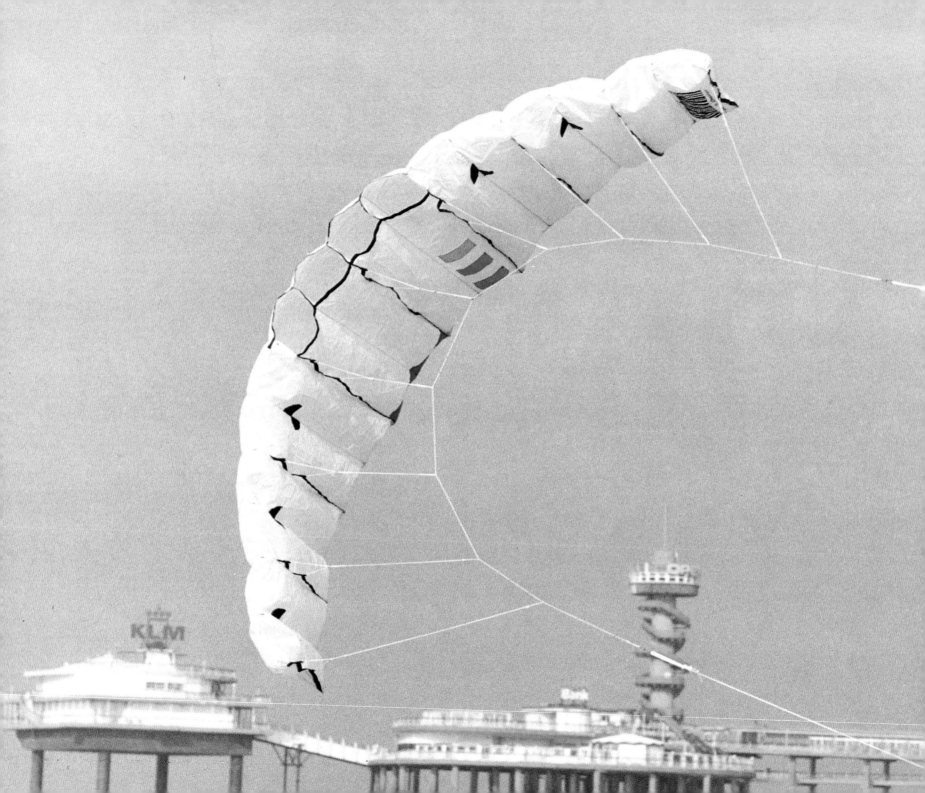

7. Following is one of the basic movements of team flying. Here with two Team-Lights.

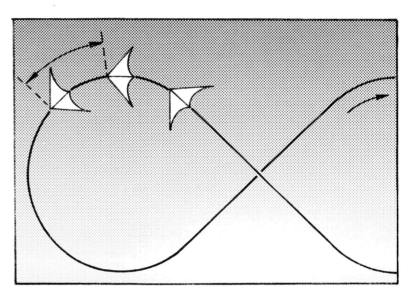

8.1 Horizontal figure eight ('infinity', mind the correct spacing).

TEAM FLYING TECHNIQUES

Let's say you have built a number of stunt kites, you have been flying them fervently for at least one season, and you think that now you have mastered these sky racers quite nicely. You can already fly dead-straight paths, fly square angles blindly and dive safely only to pull up some ten centimetres above the ground. And then comes the day that you get an invitation to join one of these spectacular stunt teams. A day not easily forgotten; suddenly there are so many things you have to think of at the same time that now and then you may mistake left for right, and fly completely in the wrong direction like an ugly duckling, or worse, even dive straight into the ground. And when you think "I'll exercise this all by myself first", you forget that this sort of exercising can only be done within a team. Dual-flying may be an amusing thing to do, but team flying with three or four other flyers offers many more possibilities. This book unfortunately cannot help you in finding the right combination of people for a team. You should reckon with the possibility of being called all sorts of names during the super-concentrated activity of team flying when, instead of carrying out the simple maneuver of turning up, you turn down. And yet, when the routine is over and every kite is safely on the ground, all are good friends again.

STARTING UP

During the first few flying-sessions a new team will pick up a number of habits which can hardly be dropped or changed later on. Who is the leader, who follows him or her as the number-two flyer, who is third, etc. On the ground the pilots will stand beside each other in the same order. You can choose between left or right for the position of the leader. However, in the figures shown in this book the righthand pilot is the leader with kite number one. Under all circumstances each pilot should stand as close to the others as possible. Especially when the lines are crossing each other, it is of great importance to keep this crossing-angle as small as you can. As long as flyers and kites stay close together, they can frolic and rollick freely (although this had better be left to the kites!). At least some five wrap-ups are possible with good Spectra lines; however, if one of the team members makes a too fierce steering movement, or if he steers too far off, the twists in the line will eventually be really tied up and the maneuverability is absolutely gone.

What happens exactly in team flying? The various kites will fly in a certain interrelation, the *formation*, which starts in a very simple manner as a kind of 'just follow the leader' pattern. Later on joint maneuvers are flown, such as loops and squares, which are called 'synchronic flying'. After these, the asynchronic patterns will logically follow: turning away from each other, flying between and across each other's paths, followed by the complicated interlacing or *wicker work*.

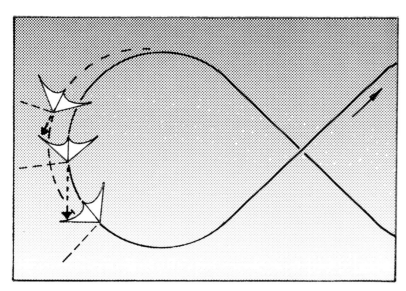

8.2 Corrections during horizontal figure eight.

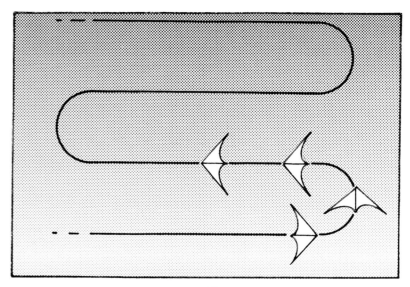

8.3 Ladder.

STAGE 1: FOLLOWING

It is quite an obvious thing to just follow in the track of the leader. But when you are only engaged in chasing his 'rear-end', the sharpness of the said pattern is soon lost. Small flight corrections made by the leader will soon result in ever greater deviations by the followers. It boils down to constantly trying to compromise between pure following and independently flying the planned pattern. Keep wondering whether the kite leading you is only making slight flight corrections or whether it has really started going round the corner. There is a strong tendency for the following kites to cut off wide turns, which causes the whole bunch to fly closer to each other, ending up in shambles as a result. The trick is not to keep hanging right behind the kite leading you, but to direct your nose at his outercurve wing.

The first flight routine of a beginners' team, and at the same time the ideal warming-up for any team, is flying a horizontal figure eight, called *infinity*. A great advantage of this pattern is its continuity without a beginning nor an end. It will serve as the basis and the approach path of patterns to follow and also as a 'receptacle' after any flopped exercises. It consists of two three quarter circles connected by two straight lines, crossing each other right in the centre. The flight direction is important: always slantingly upwards through the centre, for that is the point with the highest wind-force. Descending is done in the outside-bends. Thus the flying speed will remain constant. The largest number of kites that we have flown through the horizontal figure eight was twelve. A greater number may well be possible, but do not forget that all kites must have passed the point of intersection before the first one arrives at this point again.

For a good looking line of kites following each other, equal *spacing* is a must. Spacing here means that the distance between the first and the second kite must be equal to the space between the second and the third, the third and the fourth, and so on. This implies that one has to learn to keep an eye on all kites at the same time, whereas the steering of one's own kite becomes automatic. It does happen that you lose your bearings; you will find yourself steering a kite for some time that is not attached to your own lines. Optimum spacing is dependent on the pattern flown, but for most of the patterns a minimal distance of a full wingspan between the leader and the follower is necessary. How to keep up the right spacing?

Most of the time you are in imminent danger of passing the kite before you. You can prevent this by taking the turns somewhat wider; this looks better and because of the longer path chosen, the spacing increases automatically. By taking a few steps forwards or backwards the kite can be easily accelerated or slowed down. But never forget that the pilot following you must also react to these variations in speed. Therefore try to keep your speed as constant as possible. If you keep having spacing problems it is high time to change the kite's speed by adjusting its bridle. Try to bridle the whole line of kites in such a way that the forerunner (number one) has optimum bridling, number two slightly slower, the third one again somewhat slower, and so on.

When the infinity is performed smoothly, it will be time to try and fly some square corners too. Keep an eye on the kite before you in particular. As soon as you see it go around the corner, punch an imaginary thumb-tack in the sky right at the spot of its turning point and fly around this thumb-tack yourself before following it again.

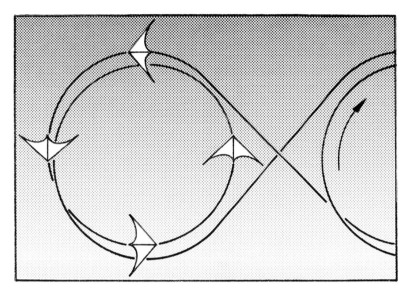

8.4 Wrapping up/unwrapping.

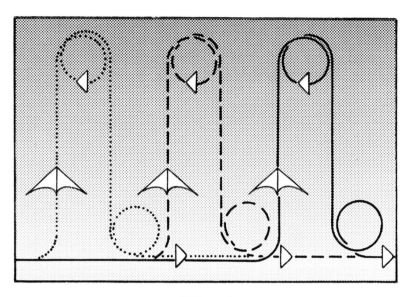

8.5 Paper clip.

Exercises in following

Ladder
– leader keeps up fixed course
– spacing
– keep flying well into the very ends

Wrap up/unwrap
– keep the kites close
– during the wrapping distribute the kites evenly around the circle.

STAGE 2: PARALLEL EXECUTION OF SYMMETRICAL PATTERNS

Again we start out from the infinity. The moment that all kites are on the straight path, the team leader will give the command for all to start turning a left loop. When everybody turns a similar loop and the spacing is more than a wingspan, there will be no incidents. The right path can be continued and on the next straight the twists are removed from the lines by turning a right loop.

A lot depends on the commands of the leader. For the same reasons as is the case with military commands, these should consist of two parts: "Turn...Now!", or "Left loop...Now!". The first part is the announcement, after which there is an interval of half a second, followed by the actual command to start the movement. After having gained some experience the whole team will be familiar with the routine, so that the first part of the command can be left out, the second part sufficing. With loops carried out so close to each other, everybody has to make the turn at the same speed and with the same diameter. There will be enough time for corrections during the turn itself, small steps forward or backward are very useful now. Keep a very good eye on your neighbors. After some dozens of exercises you will notice that everybody has adapted himself to the whole team and the loops become quite synchronic. The band of riotous pilots has, indeed, begun to turn into a stunt team.

Exercising parallel patterns

Paper clip
1. From the left come in horizontally and low.
2. "And...Turn!": climb up synchronically on this command.
3. "Loop right...Now!": fly 1½ circle.
4. Fly straight down until just above the ground.
5. "Loop left...Now!": fly 1¼ circle.
6. Fly horizontally to the right.

A crucial factor in this pattern is a parallel downward flight. If you fly in the direction of the ground unequally, the second loop will be a mess. With all team members walking a good deal forwards simultaneously during the down-flight, the speed will be less, leaving you more time for corrections. The leader will of course watch out that nobody has plunged his kite into the turf before giving the command "Loop left".

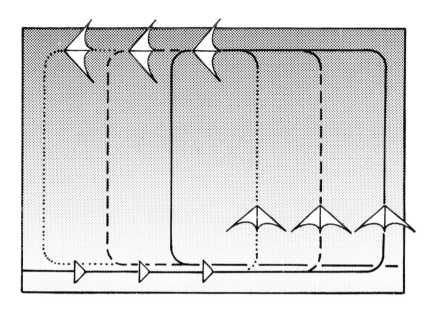

8.6 Squares.

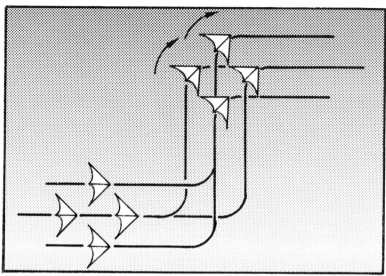

8.7 Diamond formation.

Squares

1. From the left come in horizontally and low.
2. "And...Turn!": climb in parallel paths.
3. "And...Turn!": fly to the left in reverse order.
4. "And...Turn!": descend in parallel paths.
5. "And...Turn!": fly away horizontally at the same height, as in nr. 1.

The most difficult part is the horizontal path in the top part of the square. Here the leader comes last, which means that he has to deal with a lot of foul wind from his forerunners. Create ample spacing to minimize this effect.

Diamond Formation

There are various ways to form this diamond. For example, coming from the left, lined up, number two starts flying slightly higher, number three somewhat lower, number four accelerates and links up with the leader. So as to maintain the formation as long as possible, all pilots walk forwards, thus regulating the kites' speed properly and hence the shape of the formation. The two square turns in the pattern should be taken cautiously, so that the kites keep flying on at a constant speed.

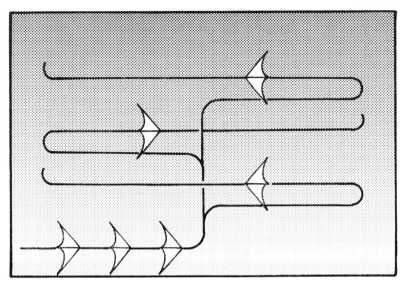

8.8 Split.

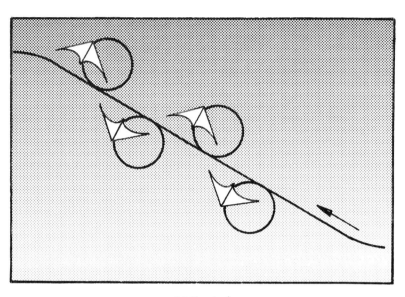

8.9 Counter-loops.

STAGE 3: MIRROR FLYING

This implies patterns in which the kites are flying away from each other. The thrill involved in this pattern is at the point where the kites, having flown towards each other again, just manage to avoid colliding with their counterparts.

Exercising mirror flying

Split

Again we start out flying from the horizontal figure eight, flying just over the ground and up in the centre. This is where the Split starts.

1. "Split...Now!": the even-numbered kites go right, the odd-numbered ones go left.
2. "And...Turn!": at the edge of the wind-window make a 180° turn.
3. Pass each other exactly in the centre.
4. "Turn!": make the same kind of turn again at the edge.
5. "Merge...Now!": start merging just before the centre point.

This is an easy but spectacular pattern, which can be extended with loops at the moment of passing; the more kites, the better! See to it that during the fly-out the even and odd kites keep flying at mutually the same speed and height; also, that at the turning-points the turn is made upwards, without gaining height. So, even when several flights to and fro are made, each kite will remain in its own path. The command "Merge...Now!" should be given in time, so as to prevent the kites from flying on, but make them climb up exactly in line.

Counter-loops

1. Just keep on flying the infinity with long straight paths.
2. "And...Turn!": numbers one and three rotate to the right, numbers two and four rotate to the left.
3. After the loops keep on flying the infinity.
4. "And...Turn!": numbers two and four will now rotate to the right, one and three to the left.

Here too the advice is: repeat the exercise often, for you have to get used to the movement of falling again into the follow-me formation after having finished the loops.

STAGE 4: THE ROUTINE

When finally the team masters the above patterns, the moment has come to think of a genuine routine. A routine is a sequence of a number of blending flying-patterns. We will give you an example of a pattern, but then the moment is there for you to start making them up yourself. After a while the team will have a dozen or more different patterns on its repertoire, which it may find hard to memorize. Try to combine various 'moves' that blend easily and memorize them as one pattern. These 'lumps' can then be moulded easily into one complete routine by means of infinities connecting them. The routine serves a two-fold purpose. In the first place it will help you remember all the moves the team has developed. Secondly, the team is building up a well-finished programme for competitions and demonstrations, complete with starts and landings.

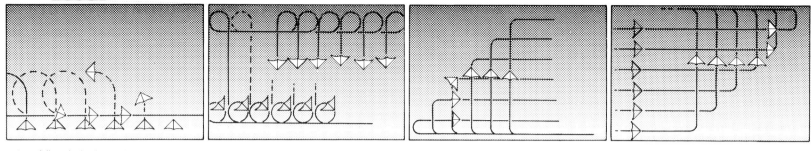

1. *Start, follow the leader one by one.* 2. *Parallel square with loops.* 3. *Domino turns, right.* 4. *Domino turns, left.*

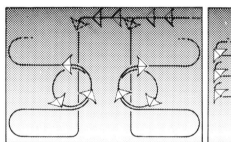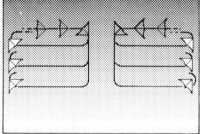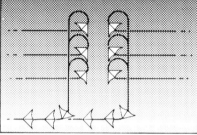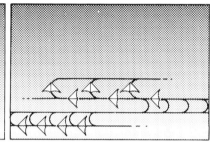

5. *Mirror image wrap, 3 by 3.* 6. *Horizontal split.* 7. *Bump-loop up, line up at ground level.* 8. *Parallel ladder up, uneven jump out.*

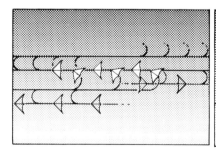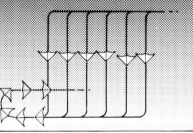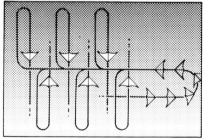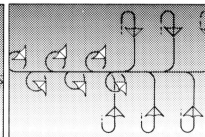

9. *Even jump in, continue ladder up.* 10. *Powerdive.* 11. *Vertical cross-over, 3 times.* 12. *Line-up left, contra loops.*

9. *A part of the precision routine as flown by the Dike Hoppers during the world cup 1991 in Bristol, England.*

7 THE COLLECTION

We can easily imagine that by now your fingers are itching to build such a super stunter yourself. But the question is, which one? This is a matter of thinking it over thoroughly first before you lock yourself up with your sewing machine. Two questions must be answered beforehand: what is it you want to do with the kite, and where do you live? If you live far from the beach, a lightwind stunter should be your choice, because even under less favorable conditions the kite will take to the air. Should you be in a position to use the beach, the wind limitations generally do not apply and you only have to formulate exactly what you want to do with the kite. Below we give a description of eleven kite models which will undoubtedly enable you to make a well thought-out choice.

SHUTTLE

The Shuttle is a variant of the well-known Ace (also called Trilby or Acroracer). It is an uncomplicated kite of the familiar diamond type, capable of flying in 4 to 8 Beaufort winds. Especially with a tail it is an attractive looking kite. It is an ideal kite to learn stunt kiting, and indestructible too. All accessories are to be had in the kite shops. Its pull is low; hence it is the best kite to put into a child's hands. Very easy to stack, trains of more than two hundred Aces have been flown successfully. A standard Ace is of the same height and width; for this book we designed a wider kite - which stays in better shape in strong winds - the Shuttle.

SPEEDWING

An easy to build stunt delta without a central spine. Formidable speed, pull and maneuverability. The heavier models are practically indestructible. Operational from 2 Beaufort, but especially exciting above 3 Beaufort. Easy to stack. Not fit for children under 12. It is the ideal model for a beginning stunt flyer. Bridling is very sensitive, the difference between good and disastrous is within a few millimetres. An enlarged version of the Speedwing is particularly suited for heavy-duty jobs, like skiing over the beach.

Since certain aspects of the Speedwing are patented the kite may only be built for your private use.

The Speedwing is a poor choice for team-flying because of its nervous steering qualities. However, flown in stacks of three, the Speedwing appears to be a spectacular team-kite, but beware of its strong pull.

TEAM-LIGHT

A featherweight variant of the Hawaiian. The craze of delta-stunting was set off by the Hawaiian, a design of Don Tabor (Top of the Line-Kites). The Hawaiian needs less wind than other stunt kites in order to get started properly. It can be firmly steered with good turning behaviour. It does show a tendency to drop down when made to loop too tight. Produces a very strong pull, noticeably more than the Standard-200 (cf. below). Flies from 2 Beaufort to 6. Not easy to build. The variant described here (Team-Light) is of a very light construction and so it is capable of flying as from 1 Beaufort. Of all the types described in this book, this is the best team-kite for minimal wind conditions.

STANDARD-200

A stunt kite of basic delta shape. From 2 Beaufort to 6 it is the most all-round kite you may wish. Highly maneuverable and capable of making quick, tight loops and turns, with clean-cut lines. The Standard-200 is essentially a fast and hard-pulling model, but it can easily be made fit for team flying. Because of its simple construction and its hardly critical adjustment, this model is, next to the Speedwing, most suitable for the beginner. Yet, due to its size and vulnerability (our version is executed in 6 mm carbon), some experience in stunt kiting is desirable.

KWAT

For those who prefer something quite different: a four-line stunter of our own design. It can be flown forwards, in reverse, hang on one spot and spin like a propeller. It has no excessive speed or pull, but it is more a matter of 'delicately moving the kite around'. Simple to construct and bridle, robustly built, the kite can easily stand the inevitable emergency landings.

CICADA AND GIZMO

Dutch variants of a modern French design (Big Brother) with an elongated central spine. Lightly built, the Cicada can be flown as from 1 Beaufort to 5. The Gimzo is usable from 2 Beaufort to 7. Especially suited to team flying because even at increasing wind-forces its pull remains relatively low. These are the best maneuverable of all the dual-line kites described in this book, with perfect control right into the farthest corners of the window. There is but little flapping of the sail due to the smoothly curved trailing edges of the wings, combined with the tensioned wing tip. Therefore these are rather quiet kites. Gizmo and Cicada are actually similar types: the Gizmo is based on frame material of 1.5 metres length, the larger Cicada is built up of carbon parts of 1.65 metres (or 82.5 cm). They are slightly more difficult to build than the Standard-200.

SPEEDFOIL

An extremely fast cousin of the Flexifoil. The Speedfoil can be firmly steered, but it is less maneuverable than the deltawings. It will fly from 2 Beaufort to 8, but it is especially exciting from 4 Beaufort onwards. This kite is really like a dragster and very simple to stack. Do-it-yourself-construction is difficult and only reserved for those with both experience and patience. It is practically indestructible. The conical fibre rod is to be had in kite-shops.

For the very reason that the Speedfoil is capable of making wide and smooth turns, this kite is certainly suitable as a team model. This model too is protected by certain patents and may only be copied for your private use.

SPUTNIK 1 & 2

Home designs, for the connoisseur. Sputnik 1 is a sparless kite, capable of developing an incredible pull in strong winds and therefore absolutely unfit for team flying. The hardly smaller Sputnik 2 is also a sparless kite, with exceptional maneuverability and a relatively low pull in strong winds. Under such circumstances the ideal kite for team flying.

DYKEHOPPER

This slim model, nicknamed *The Crate* or *The Beast*, is actually out of place in this book, or rather thrown in as an extra. If you really think that you have mastered the art of building stunt kites, then this is your testcase. The Beast is hard to build, even harder to trim and diabolical to fly. In the first instance the kite was designed for the stunt flying team the *Dike Hoppers*. Steering is extremely precise and the creating of *stacks* (i.e. hooking up several kites in the air, as if they are connected in train-formation) goes off fantastically. Loops look great - as if one wingtip is nailed to the sky. Unfortunately, the kite's unstable behaviour at launching and the very critical bridling makes the Dykehopper unfit for serious team flying. But should you be looking for excitement and for extreme pull, this is your kite.

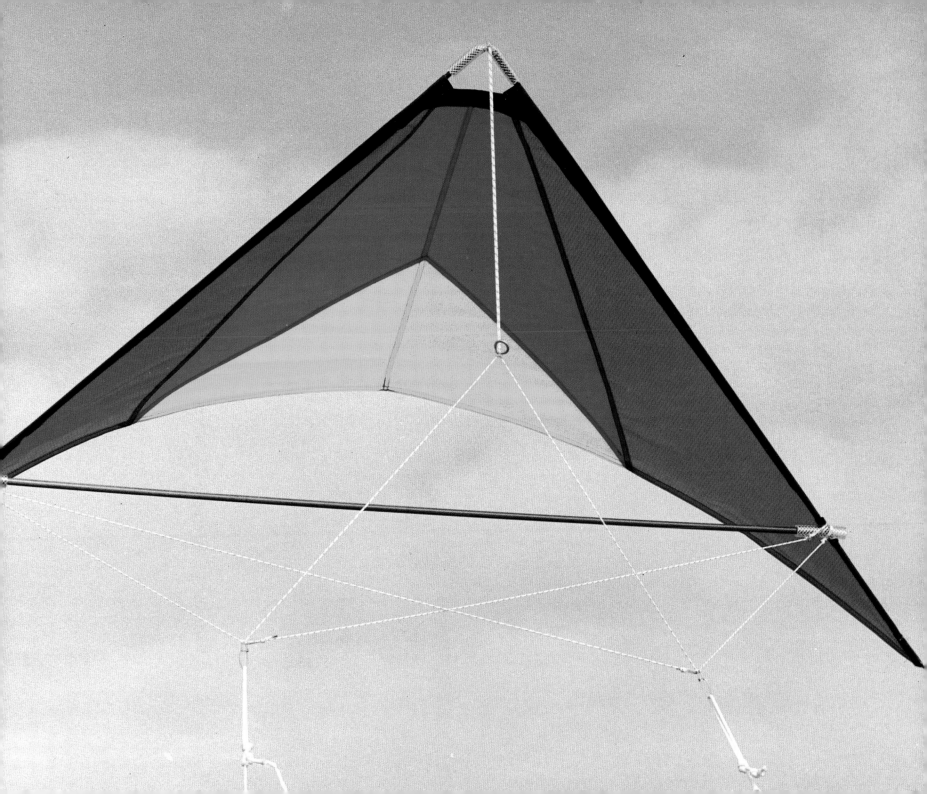

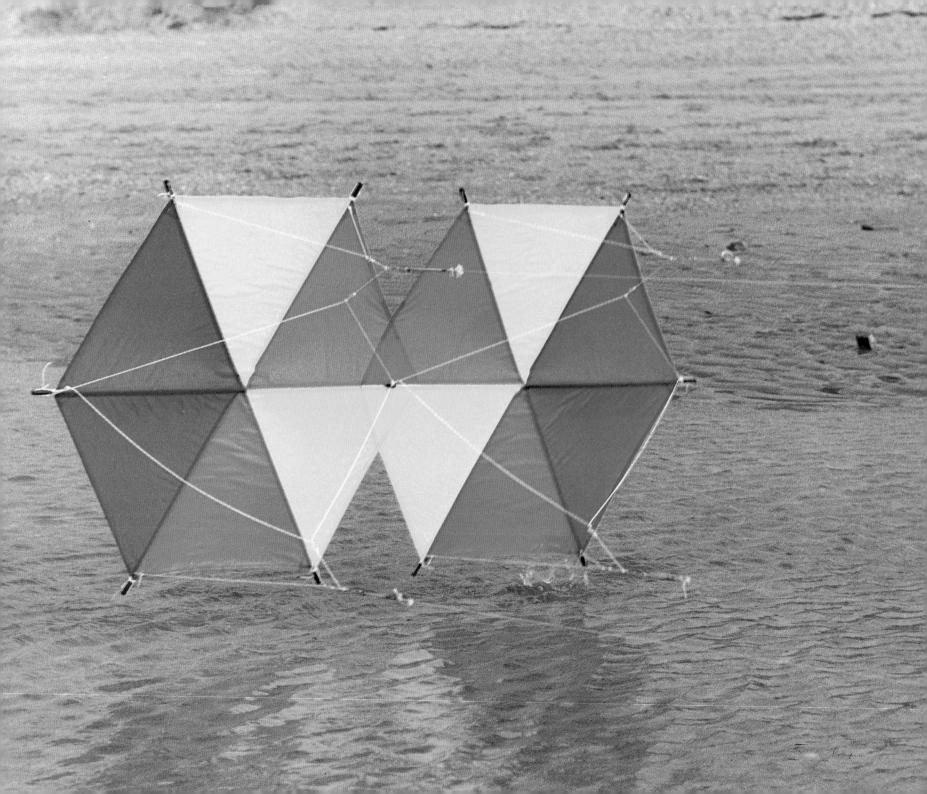

8 BUILDING KITES, A BASIC COURSE

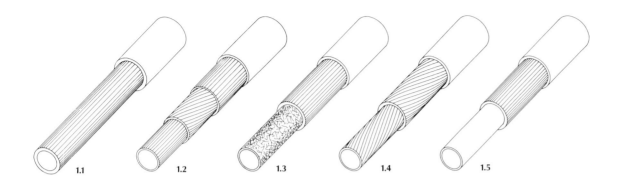

1 Carbon tubes:
1. Uni-directional carbon.
2. 20 percent of the fibres wound around.
3. Core of randomly directed fibres.
4. Two layers of fibres rotating in opposite directions at a slight angle.
5. Carbon with an aluminum core.

Suppose you have never made a kite before. You haven't got a clue what spinnaker nylon is, you have never held a carbon rod and look puzzled when Kevlar tape comes up for discussion. No problem, in half an hour from now you will know everything.

Some people are still making kites consisting of an arc made up of pieces of wood, some twine and kite-paper. One hour of rigging up, put the tail on and there it goes. Cheap and pure kiting, as in the early days.

Stunt kite flyers are less nostalgic. Stunt kites are made of the lightest and strongest materials available nowadays. This fact makes it possible to go stunting comfortably at a wind-force of 1 Beaufort, while the same kite will remain in good shape at 4 Beaufort.

FRAME MATERIAL

Traditional material for supporting kite shapes is, of course, wood. In the old days perhaps square sticks of steamed beech, today tropical ramin spars. This material is not very suitable for stunt kites, except in special cases, such as 6 mm ramin in sail spars or trains of small stunt-deltas with well-balanced forces.

The first improvement on wood was bamboo. Bamboo has a lower weight per metre than wood, it is stiffer and shows more resistance against fracture. The problem with bamboo is that it is hard to get in one and the same quality. Its qualities are not even homogeneous over the length of one bamboo stalk. This material is therefore unserviceable for a manufacturer of stunt kites, but a patient do-it-yourself builder might try it out.

SYNTHETICS

The good characteristics and structure of bamboo have been imitated in synthetic tubes, basically resins reinforced by strong longitudinal fibres. There are many types of fibre, but their use as material for kites is limited to glassfibre and carbon fibre. A popular name for glassfibre is RF (reinforced fibre), whereas carbon fibre is also known as RCF (reinforced carbon fibre). Synthetics used to keep these tubes in proper shape are polyester, acrylate, vinylester or epoxy (in order of increasing quality).

When choosing the materials for the frame you should pay attention to three properties:
Weight is usually expressed in a number of grammes per metre of material. The thickness of the walls is of considerable influence on this number of grammes. Secondly, the kind of material: carbon fibre is approx. 20 percent lighter than glassfibre.
Rigidity is the material's resistance to bending. We have measured this factor for materials mostly used, by clamping the rod at one side and by loading it with weights at a distance of 70 cm. Rigidity is then formulated in Newton per centimetre of bending. Rigidity increases dramatically with the diameter of the tubing. Twice as thick is roughly eight times as stiff. Yet the diameter of stunt kite material is limited to some 10 mm, exceptionally to 12 mm, because vulnerability greatly increases with larger diameters. Any gain in rigidity had better be scored from the use of carbon fibre. At equal diameters a carbon fibre tube is three times as stiff as glassfibre tubing on the average.
Crash resistance is a property not easily expressed in figures. Solid glassfibre and carbon fibre material is practically unbreakable, hence especially suited for small stunt kites. Although the frames of these kites don't require great stiffness, they must be capable of sustaining many and strong shocks. In this respect kites suitable for beginners and children, are models such as the Peter Powell and the Shuttle, but also half-size models of the Gizmo, for example.

So as to improve the stability of its shape, not all fibres of tubing-material are running unidirectionally, as is the case with arrow shafts. As much as 20 percent of the fibres can be wrapped around, or, as with the RF and RCF tubes, a core with randomly directed fibres is applied. Top quality carbon fibre tube is built up from two layers of fibres, running in opposite directions under a slight angle. A particularly fine variant is the alu-carbon construction with the core made up of very thin-walled aluminum tubing.

Metric system. All measures supplied in this book are part of the metric system. Unless specifically stated otherwise, the measures given in the construction plans (cf. page 54 and beyond) are in centimetres. In order to prevent inaccuracies in the English version of this book, we did not convert these measures into the imperial system.

Things are slightly more complicated in the case of frame material measures. At present

fibre rod (solid)	weight gr/m	rigidity Newton/cm
glass		
F 2	6	-
F 3	13	0.01
F 4	24	0.04
F 5	37	0.10
F 6	54	0.20
carbon		
CF 2	5	0.01
CF 3	10	0.03
CF 4	18	0.14

fibre tube (hollow)	weight gr/m	rigidity Newton/cm
glass		
RF 6	28	0.18
RF 8	41	0.53
RF 9	48	0.77
RF 10	50	0.90
RF 12	65	1.51
carbon		
RCF 6	22	0.50
RCF 8	32	1.35
RCF 9	35	1.83
RCF 10	40	2.80
RCF 11	45	3.85

arrow material (82,5 cm)	weight gr/m	rigidity Newton/cm
glass/epoxy		
A 7.6 mm	27	0.30
B 8.9 mm	34	0.55
unidirectional carbon fibre		
5.5 mm	18	0.40

there exists no worldwide standard for carbon fibre and fibreglass tubes. External and internal diameters are variable, and so are the wall gauges, the material used, the fibre winding system and what have you. For the kites in this book we started out with a collection of synthetic composite tubes with external diameters increasing by 2 mm, hence tubes of 2, 4, 6, 8, 10, 12 and 14 mm external' and a wall-thickness of 1 mm. From the chart given, you will note the rigidity of all these tubes and their weight per metre. With this chart you will be in a position to choose a tube in your kite shop with rigidity approaching our data.

In this book we mostly use 6 mm carbon fibre tubing as frame material. You can substitute this type of material by 5.5 mm carbon fibre arrow shafts. These arrow shafts are more vulnerable than the 6 mm tubing which have been developed for stunt kites. In Appendix 9 (cf. page 96) you will find a conversion-table together with some suggestions.

How to use the charts. With the help of the following information, the weight of a frame can be determined. The weight of the rods or tubes is actually the most important factor of the total weight.

As a rule of thumb we assume: a kite weighing less than 300 gr/m^2 is a light-wind kite, one from 300-450 gr/m^2 is a medium-wind kite, one over 450 gr/m^2 is a strong-wind kite.

Let us look at the Standard-200 as an example:

	RCF 6 tube	RF 8 tube
complete sail	100 gram	100 gram
various parts	50 gram	50 gram
5.5 meter of tube	120 gram	225 gram
total	270 gram	375 gram
on a surface of 0.73 m²	370 gram/m²	510 gram/m²

It is obvious that the right choice of frame material makes a great difference with regard to the final product: either a good average kite or a distinctly heavy model! And all this at practically the same rigidity!

With the help of the charts the rigidity of combined tubing is easily calculated by totalling the separate rigidities. For example, in the case of the Speedwing cross-strut of 6 mm RCF, reinforced with an 8 mm RF tube: 0.50 + 0.53 = 1.03 N/cm. Doubling the stiffness is a handy method to reinforce your kite on the flying-site in case of a sudden freshening wind.

Connection parts. Every now and then frame-parts must be connected. In almost all models of stunt kites the lower spreader consists of two parts, whilst in certain cases the wing spars are divided to make transport easier.

Epoxy arrow material with 20 percent glassfibre winding can be connected internally. For safety reasons all RF and RCF tubing must be connected by external connectors. These bushes usually have 0.5 mm thin brass walls. Hardened aluminum is clearly lighter and hence preferable. The total length of a bush like that must be at least ten times the diameter of the tube to be connected. So 8 mm RF tube must be connected by a bush of at least 8 centimetres in length.

It is important to round off the edges of the bush in order to prevent fracture on that spot. So as to ensure a properly centred bush at the transition of the two RF tubes, apply dual-component glue to one side. This is not advisable in the case of the lower spreader; instead,

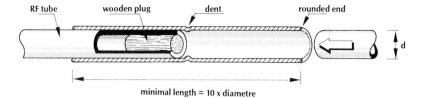

RF tube · wooden plug · dent · rounded end

minimal length = 10 x diametre

2. The way to connect two lengths of tubing.

3. Vinyl tube. Non-reinforced as retainers (black rings), reinforced as cross-fittings.

make a small dent above and below the half-way point of the bush. We advise you to glue small wooden plugs in the RF and RCF tube-ends, in order to prevent their splitting.

Recently we noted more and more synthetic connectors, mainly as lower-spreader connectors with a built-in spine-connector (cf. Gizmo construction plan).

One last remark and warning regarding your kite frame: caution! Glassfibre and carbon fibre tubes are easily damaged. When they lie on the ground and you step on them accidentally, they may crack internally and invisibly, which may eventually result in broken frames while kiting.

Be careful with shattered pieces too; in any case see to it that these awful splinters are not left behind on the kiting-site. Care must also be taken when working with glassfibre. To prevent inhaling its saw dust you had better saw the material near the mouthpiece of a running vacuum cleaner, or even under a running water tap. The minute glassfibre particles may be harmful for the lungs. On the skin they produce a prickling feeling which disappears after some time. As far as we know this has no permanent ill effects.

VINYL TUBE

Most connections between the various frame parts are made with PVC tube, more widely known as vinyl tube. It is available in two types: reinforced and non-reinforced. The former type contains a web of woven reinforcing threads causing the tube to become stiffer and stronger. From the non-reinforced type the rings are usually cut, which are glued on the frame so as to keep cross-fittings and T-fittings in their places. Vinyl tube is to be had in all

sorts of inner and outer diameters.

The best way of making holes in vinyl is with the help of an electric or manual drill. Use a small hollow pipe or a piece of brass tube with a diameter 1 mm less than the rod it should contain. It is not necessary to sharpen the edges of the brass tube, a blunt piece of tube can also be lowered into the vinyl in a couple of seconds.

KITE-SAIL MATERIAL

SPINNAKER NYLON

A stunt kite is made of spinnaker nylon. A spinnaker is a bulging front sail on a sailing boat, which is hoisted at quarterly-wind and down-wind courses. Spinnaker nylon was first developed for these sails: it is lightweight, windproof, low-stretch and has a network of reinforcing threads (hence the English name of 'ripstop nylon').

For the manufacture of spinnaker nylon first a web is woven of horizontal and vertical nylon threads: warp and woof. Then the nylon threads are heated and rolled. This procedure is called calendering. The temperature during calendering determines the characteristics of the nylon cloth. When the cloth is strongly heated, the nylon threads will melt partly and stick together. The cloth feels stiff and paperlike with minimal stretch. It is relatively susceptible to tear.

A lower degree of heating results in a much softer and elastic cloth. The nylon fibres are hardly damaged, the cloth can stretch properly and is more tear-resistant.

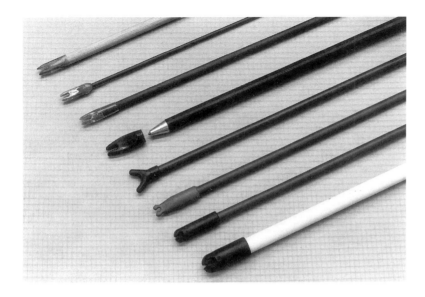

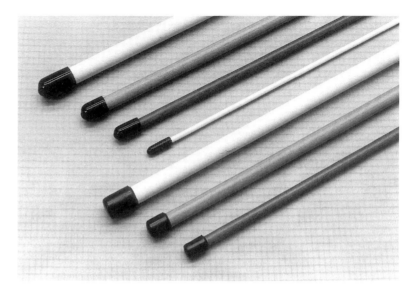

The degree to which it is windproof and free of stretch depends, in particular, on the coating of the cloth, apart from the heating and rolling. This coating mostly consists of polyurethane, sometimes of silicones. You can find this out by simply pressing a piece of sellotape on the cloth. If it stays on, the cloth has a polyurethane coating. If the sellotape falls off the cloth, silicones have been used.

It appears that each roll of spinnaker nylon is different, even if it is of the same color and has been made by the same factory. Especially the stretch diagonal on the direction in which the cloth is woven varies with each roll. Spinnaker cloth with the least possible diagonal stretch is the most pleasant material to work with, producing the finest kites. Therefore, look carefully at the stability of the cloth when choosing this material; the color is secondary.

Talking about colors, yellow and fluorescent pink appear to be most sensitive to ultraviolet rays. The colors will fade and the cloth will become brittle. And to make things even more complicated: apart from the coating, color and heat treatment, the weight of the cloth also plays a prominent role. 32-gram and 65-gram nylon cloths are easily obtainable. For our purpose 32-gram cloth is generally used, the 65-gram type being reserved for exceptional cases (e.g. for large kites and as reinforcement pieces).

DACRON FABRIC

Polyester fabric is usually sold under the name of Dacron. Dacron is stiffer, stronger and heavier than spinnaker nylon. It is mainly used for leading-edge sleeves and reinforcement pieces. Dacron is to be had both in rolls of 1 or 1.5 metre width and in the shape of band (in various widths). Dacron weighs 100 to 200 gram/m^2. Dacron is to be handled in the same way as spinnaker nylon.

KEVLAR FABRIC

Kevlar is the brand name for aramide fibres (cf. the chapter on control lines). Kevlar fabric is extremely strong, no sharp rod or strut is capable of piercing Kevlar fabric in case of a collision. For that reason Kevlar band (which is, in fact, Kevlar fabric cut in strips) is particularly suited to reinforce the ends of leading-edge sleeves. Kevlar is always yellowish of color.

WEBBING

Kevlar band as such is hard to get, whereas it is quite easy to obtain seat belt webbing. This material has the same function but is to be had in various colors, it is thicker and heavier too. Webbing is usually applied as the last protective layer on the nose of a delta stunter.

BUNGEE CORD

The kite-sail is tensioned by elastic. We distinguish bungee cord from waist-belt elastic which is a wide type of elastic band particularly suited to be pulled over wing spars so as to keep the spar under tension inside the seam. Bungee cord is mostly used at the wingtips where it is pinched in an arrow nock. Both types of elastic are to be had in various gauges and colors.

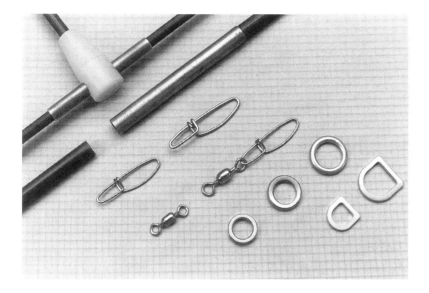

4. Arrow nocks.
5. Soft (top) and hard end caps.
6. T-fitting (top), clips (centre) and rings.

ACCESSORIES

The industry has marketed accessories specially meant for stunt kiting. Thus you have a fine nylon T-fitting connecting the 6 mm spine of a Standard-200 (cf. its description) easily with the brass tube holding the two lower struts. There are also neatly finished arrow nocks fitting over the ends of the wing spars; the bungee cord fits snugly in.

Because the assortment of accessories is changing from day to day, we can hardly supply you with an extensive list of them. So a visit to one of the specialized kite-shops in your area will put you wise.

THE CONSTRUCTION

In the following chapters we will supply an extensive construction plan for each type of kite. Here are some useful tips for the construction of all stunt kites:
1. You should have a large working-table with sufficient lighting, free of grease or dirt, of approx. 1.2 by 2.0 metres. Keep a piece of hardboard or cardboard at hand to put on the table when you have to heat or cut something.
2. Always make a template of half a kite. Consult each construction plan to find out whether the measures given for the template include a hem or not.
3. Sometimes it is handy to make two templates: one with so-called clean measures (the kite's measures after hemming) and another with the kite's measures and those of the hems added to them. The second template will be slightly larger, and you can put it

directly on the cloth to have it cut out. Then put the template with the clean measures on the spinnaker cloth and outline it with a pencil. You have to put the various parts together right on this pencil line (cf. points 8 and 9 in the sewing tips hereafter). This method saves you a lot of time when you have to draw and cut the same parts of a kite a couple of times (such as the wing profiles of a Speedfoil and the twelve identical parts of the Kwat).
4. Pay due attention to the indication given about the grain of the spinnaker cloth. Generally speaking, the template should be placed in such a manner on the cloth that the grain is squared on the trailing edge of the kite. Should the grain be diagonal on the trailing edge, this edge will stretch considerably and your kite will be a noisy, flapping and slow object. In each construction plan we will indicate the best way to put the templates on the cloth. This will automatically give you the correct grain, which fact will also ensure economical use of the cloth.
5. In addition to the standard utensils such as a pair of scissors, a hacksaw, a Stanley knife, short and long rulers, a drill, files, a triangle and pencil, a so-called 'hot-knife' comes in handy to construct your first stunt kite. A soldering iron of at least 50 Watt could also be used for this purpose if you sharpen the tip a little.
6. Whether your kite will be successful or not depends on the accuracy of the template. Do not fiddle with the measures given. Cardboard of 300 grammes or heavier is the most suitable template material. You will not meet with any problems when moving a soldering-iron along its outlines and it can easily be cut with a Stanley knife or something similar. Hardboard is also frequently used.

SEWING SPINNAKER NYLON

A spinnaker-cloth kite sail is practically always sewn on a sewing-machine. So you will have to learn that. The sewing-machine can be of a very simple type: straight forward and backward will do, zigzagging is not necessary. An electric, treadle or hand machine - anything is OK. A total beginner first has to try to sew straight, to change direction and to fix the last stitch. The best way to learn this is to try and follow the lines on squared paper with an unthreaded needle. After that you can draw fancy figures on the paper, then try to 'stitch them loose' with the threadless needle of your sewing-machine. Having done all this you should try to thread both the upper and the lower threads and lay a piece of double-folded spinnaker cloth under the pressure-foot of the machine for the first real sewing-test. A few tips:
1. It is certainly worth the effort to service your sewing-machine thoroughly before you start doing the stitching. This will take very little time and the result is a more even stitching. After cleaning the machine, first stitch some old cotton rags, which will absorb any oily remnants.

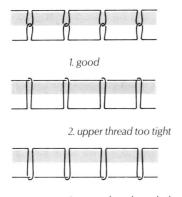

7. Adjustment of thread tension.

1. good

2. upper thread too tight

3. upper thread too slack.

2. Adjust the machine for large stitches of at least 3 mm. Small stitches will perforate the cloth.

3. The screw on the bobbin for the lower thread should be adjusted in such a manner that the bobbin will just remain hanging in the air when you let it dangle from its thread. However, when you give this thread a little tug, the bobbin should drop.

4. After having adjusted the tension of the lower thread, you will do the same with the upper thread. This should be done in such a manner that the knot the machine makes in the two threads will lie inside the double-folded spinnaker cloth. If you can see the knot on the upper side (turned towards you), the tension of the upper thread is too tight. Slacken the adjustment screw of the upper thread. However, should the knot be visible on the under side of the cloth, the tension of the upper thread should be slightly increased. Generally speaking, you should not have to touch the bobbin of the lower thread.

5. In case both the upper thread and the lower thread are too tightly adjusted, the knot might appear neatly centred inside the cloth, but the cloth will wrinkle at the seam. Especially at the places with a double seam, this doesn't look too good. Slacken both the lower and the upper threads as much as possible.

6. Th e best yarn for this work is polyester yarn which does not shrink or deteriorate when the kite gets wet. Standard gauge polyester yarn is 80. The lower this figure, the thicker the yarn. Use yarn in the same color as the spinnaker nylon as a small mistake in stitching will then hardly show. (The kites in this book have been sewn with yarns in contrasting colors so that the seams will show clearly in the pictures).

7. For normal sewing a 70 or 80 gauge needle is usual. For spots where you have to apply several layers of reinforcing material you had better use 90 or 100 gauge needles. The higher this figure, the thicker the needle. Do not be too thrifty and replace your needles in time. A needle making 'plop-plop' sounds is blunt and should be replaced. A 'plopping' needle makes too large holes in the cloth and literally drops too many stitches. Get rid of it!

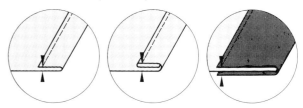

8.1 Single hem.
8.2 Double hem.
8.3 Doubled-up Dacron band around the edge of the spinnaker nylon.

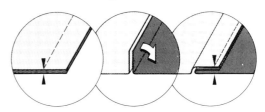

8.4 Single flat stiched seam.

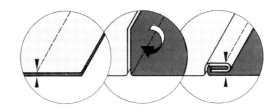

8.5 Double flat stitched seam.

8. With the exception of the stunting-wings Speedfoil and Sputnik, the stitching of stunt kites is easy: straight forward or backward, no zigzagging nor interlock. Generally, we only use three types of seams: the flat stitched seam, the normal hem and the seam connecting the sail to the leading-edge sleeves. Both the flat stitched seam and the hem can be executed single or double. Doubly-stitched they look more sophisticated, but the cloth will stretch less at the seam than the spinnaker nylon next to it. 'Bagging' becomes an imminent threat. The single hem is less prone to this phenomenon.

9. In most construction plans you are free to choose between a kite built in one color, or one with a beautiful multicolored sail. It is certainly not true that kites with a complicated pattern have worse flying characteristics than a unicolored kite; some pilots feel that they in fact fly even better, but this has never been proven.

If you want to apply a certain color-design to your kite-sail, take the following steps. First make a template according to the measures given. Make a design to scale of the sail. Then copy the design onto the template and cut it out. Copy the template-parts onto the spinnaker nylon and add 7 or 15 mm to each edge when using a single or a double flat stitched hem respectively to sew the parts together. As you will have noticed from what we said under 8., you should first lay the sail-parts on top of each other, front to front. Do this in such a way that the pencil-lines on both parts will coincide exactly; when you hold the two layers of spinnaker cloth against the light, you will see one dark line only, if properly executed. This also applies to black spinnaker cloth. Then sew the parts together on this line, as straight as possible. At the back of the kite a 7 or 15 mm wide edging of cloth will protrude. This edging must be single or double-folded to the left or the right, depending on the colors of the spinnaker cloth used. In general you had better fold the cloth-edging to the darker part of the spinnaker nylon, so that the edging is almost invisible. You can check this by again holding the kite against the light and see which color is the least transparent.

Only after having put the pattern-parts together, can you continue with the steps indicated in each construction plan. However complicated your design, take care to have the trailing edge squared on the grain of the cloth.

10. Spinnaker nylon is slippery, it will slither away from under your sewing-machine constantly. Meticulous kite builders will pre-glue difficult and important seams (on which the kite's symmetry will eventually depend). Spinnaker cloth with a polyurethane coating can be glued easily. Glue on a rubber-cement base does the job quite well; any surplus glue can be 'rolled off'. At those places where you have applied the rubbercement abundantly, spots will appear on the cloth that cannot be removed. Therefore apply thinly and preferably at those places that will disappear later under other layers of spinnaker nylon.

11. When you have to sew two pieces of spinnaker cloth over a greater length, it may happen that the one nylon layer will creep up as compared to the other. You will only notice this at the end of the seam when the two layers of cloth will end up unevenly. With regard to important seams we therefore advise you to draw pencil-lines on both parts before you start sewing them together, say at every ten centimetres or so. You should do this in such a manner that the pencil lines will be in a direct line with each other when you have sewn the parts well. Should you notice during sewing that the pencil-marks are gradually shifting, it will become obvious to you that you are again on the point of unpicking another seam. Hence the following tip.

12. When, during stitching a seam, the layers of spinnaker cloth are shifting, you can interfere as follows: grab the shifting layer and pull at it carefully, while the other layer is only moved forward by the machine's transporter. In doing so you will often succeed in ending up evenly. If not, you may cheat by doubling-up (with the help of a little knife, for instance) the excessive nylon layer just before the pressure-foot. A makeshift contrivance, but in fact you have lost to your kite!

13. Always sew the two halves of a kite in the same order. When you have started with the left half near the nose, then do the same with the right half, even if the cloth will come to lie in

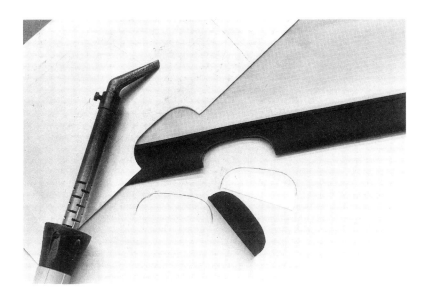

9. Soldering-iron with metal template and cardboard underlay.

an awkward position under the needle. Otherwise you will run a considerable risk of building an asymmetrical kite.

14. Usually spinnaker nylon is not cut by knife nor with scissors, but 'melted out' by means of a soldering-iron. This will prevent fraying. File a thin, flat and straight end at your soldering-iron (as you would a blunt knife); this provision will cut best.

15. Many a kite builder will use hemming-band around the edges of their kites. Never use cotton bias band for this purpose, as it will shrink terribly once the kite has become wet. Kite shops can supply you with special synthetic hemming-band.

16. Leading-edge sleeves are usually made of Dacron band. Use:
   - 5 cm Dacron band for a 6 mm frame
   - 6 cm Dacron band for an 8 mm frame
   - 7 cm Dacron band for a 9 mm frame
   - 8 cm Dacron band for a 10 mm frame.

   With these widths there will be ample space inside the leading-edge sleeves after folding and stitching. The Dacron band round the holes for the attachment of the spreaders is often a weak point with kites. Never make these holes too large, so as to have sufficient material left. Use double-gauge Dacron band around these apertures as often as possible.

SHUTTLE

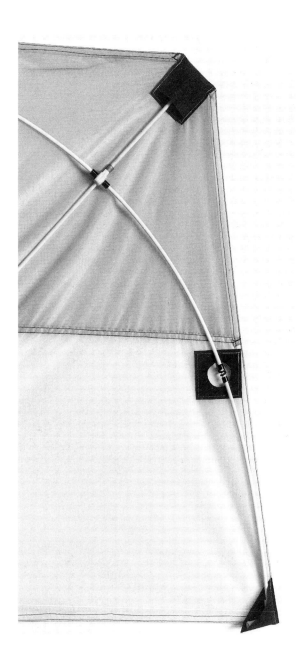

1. Easy to build and indestructible: the Shuttle.

2. Templates on the cloth,

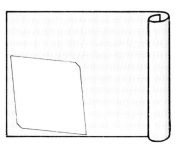 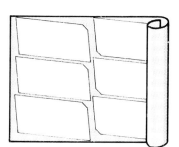

MATERIAL

0.7 m	spinnaker nylon
2.5 m	solid fibreglass 4 mm ∅
0.5 m	Dacron band 5 cm width
4 pcs	Ace end caps
1 pc	Ace cross-fitting
20 cm	vinyl tube 4 mm internal
2.5 m	thin bridle-line
	control lines of 20 kg breaking strength

TEMPLATE

Make a template according to the measures given. An all round hem of 1 cm width is already included. Put the template on the cloth and cut its shape with a soldering-iron. Pay due attention to the grain of the cloth. It will take relatively plenty of cloth when you go for a one-piece kite. Two pieces are more economical. Do not divide the sail in two parts on the spine but parallel to one of the side edges. Thus you can build three Shuttles out of 2 x 70 cm of spinnaker nylon, instead of two. In this case cut the template into the parts desired and add 1 cm to the edges that are to be stitched together. Mark your template with crosses where the three bridle fixing-points should be. Copy these points on the spinnaker cloth by putting

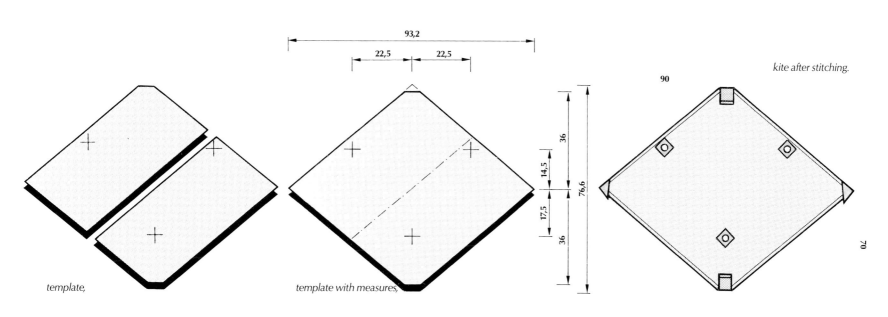

template,

template with measures,

kite after stitching.

the sail on the template; you will see the crosses shimmer through the cloth. Draw a line at 1 cm from the edge all round. Hem the kite on this line, stitching with two seams. You will now have a kite of 90 by 70 cm.

SLEEVES

With the soldering-iron cut out 4 pieces of Dacron band of 10 cm length each. Two of these pieces are meant for the spine sleeves. Double-up these pieces of band with half a centimetre difference and stitch them to the kite's back at the nose-side and the tail-side.

Double-up the other two pieces of Dacron band at 5 cm (right at the centre of the piece) and cut them off slantingly with your soldering-iron. Unfold the pieces again and stitch the single layer of Dacron at the corner. It is alright when the Dacron protrudes a little at the tail side of the corner, for the kite-sail shows a slightly sharper angle than the Dacron sleeve. Turn the remaining Dacron flap back and stitch it at the nose side only (cf. fig.4).

REINFORCEMENTS

With the soldering-iron cut out 3 pieces of Dacron band, of 5 cm length each. Stitch these three squares at the back of the kite on the spots as indicated in the drawing. Melt (from the front side of the sail) three round holes of approx. 2.5 cm; make a small wooden or metal template for this purpose.

3. The seven pieces of Dacron required, with details of the cross-strut sleeve.

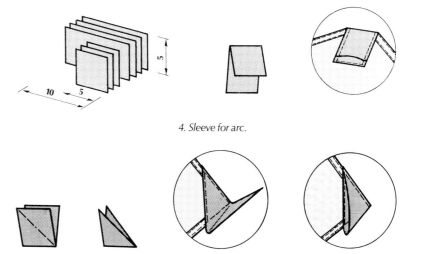

4. Sleeve for arc.

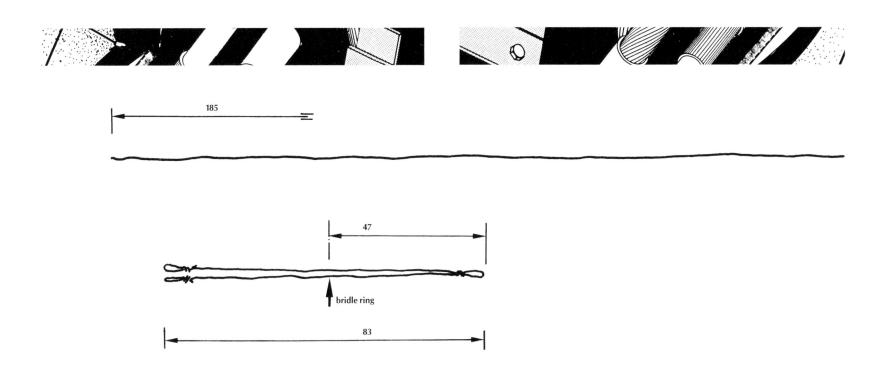

185

47

bridle ring

83

5. The bridle.

FRAME

The frame of a Shuttle consists of a glassfibre arc and a glassfibre spine. To prevent the glassfibre from quickly tearing the sleeves, special end caps have been put on the market, straight ones for the spine and rectangular ones for the arc. A special cross-fitting is to be had for the connection between spine and arc. The squared corner end cap can be replaced by shoving a 5 cm long piece of 4 mm vinyl tube onto the fibre and bending it. The straight end cap can be replaced by drilling a hole in the middle of a 4 cm long piece of 4 mm vinyl tube (through one layer of plastic) in which the fibre fits. The cross-fitting can be replaced by knotting arc and spine thoroughly together with a piece of line.

Cut 7 rings of some 5 mm width from the vinyl tube. These rings must eventually be shoved on the frame to keep the bridle and the cross-fitting in their places.

The length of the fibre arc depends on the construction method you prefer (end caps or pieces of vinyl) and on the accuracy with which you have stitched the sleeves at the corners. Saw off a piece of fibre of such a length that the fibre including end caps is 70 cm long. Shove the Ace cross-fitting, the three vinyl rings (one above the cross-fitting and two below it) and the two end caps on it. This will be the spine.

Saw off a piece of fibre of such a length that the fibre including end caps is 100 cm long. Shove the four vinyl rings and two end caps on it. This will be the arc of the kite. Put the spine into the sleeves and then the arc. Clamp the centre point of the arc into the cross-fitting and push the cross-fitting approx. 1 cm in the direction of the tailside. Thus the arc will be tightened even more and positioned exactly before the three holes in the sail, when you have done it properly. Shove the vinyl ring flush against the cross-fitting and glue the ring with ultrafast 'super-glue'.

Should the spine be too long (i.e. deep creases will show from the nose alongside the spine) or the arc too rounded (i.e. the position of the arc is above the three holes), do not hesitate to saw the fibre off. Saw off very small pieces; 3 mm will already make a great difference. A Shuttle with a too taut sail does not fly well, especially in little wind.

Mark with a pencil the spots on the fibre where the bridle should be attached. Shove the six vinyl rings left and right of the pencil marks and glue them, each ring roughly 1 cm apart. Take good care that the four rings on the arc are positioned at similar distances from the middle.

BRIDLE

Make two loops at the ends with an overhand knot. Put the loops on each other and find the middle of the line; at that point make another loop. Tie this bridle line around the spine by placing the two ends through the single loop and push the line through the hole of the kite

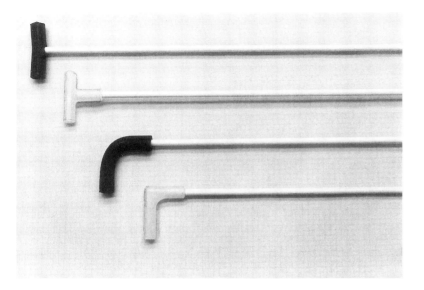

6. The end-caps of the Shuttle: the white ones are available from kite shops, the black ones are home-made.

7. Stacking Shuttles is simple.

sail. Make a larks head in both loops at the ends, remove the arc from the sleeves for a moment and shove (through the kite sail) the loops over the arc. Put the arc back into the sleeves, place the loops between the rings and pull tight.

Attach two clips or rings in the bridle at the spots indicated. The kite is ready.

TIPS

The Shuttle is especially suited to learn stunt kiting. It is indestructible, easy to build at low cost and has good flying characteristics. However, without a tail it is a nervous kite, reacting violently on control commands. Therefore it is certainly advisable to fly it with a tail in the beginning.

Ready-made tubular tails can be had in the kite shop. These are made of plastic, are inflatable and 10-15 metres long. You can construct a tail yourself, the remnants of spinnaker nylon stitched together are alright for this purpose. You can adjust its length and width as you please. Stitch a piece of Dacron where the tail begins and melt a hole in it. Put the spine through this hole (after having pulled it out of the sleeve and removed the end cap). The commercial tails also have such a reinforced piece with two holes. Push the spine from the inside through one hole. Thus the tail will open up and will fill itself with air during the flight.

This is accomplished even better when you tie a knot at the end of the tail so that the air cannot escape.

A Shuttle is stacked by means of three stacking-lines of approx. 1 metre each. Only the front one has a bridle. Should you want to stack many Shuttles, say more than six, it is advisable not to fasten the stacking-lines to the frame, but to each other. In this manner you prevent the fibre of the front kites (which have to endure the strongest forces) from being pulled to pieces. The stacking-line must be knotted to the larks head of the previous kite with another larks head. This method is only workable when you start off from the first kite (the one with a bridle) and work backwards.

With really long trains a so-called triangle is placed before the foremost kite; a 'triangle' is a triangular frame of glassfibre or carbon fibre preventing the first kite from being crushed (cf. Appendix under 5).

Shuttles in a train fly more comfortably than individually. A small train appears to take the air more easily with low wind-forces (2 to 3 Beaufort) than a single Shuttle. The front kite must be bridled a lot higher than usual, or the train will not go up. Large trains had better be composed at home, not on the beach. There is nothing as frustrating as tinkering with your Shuttle train with the sun burning on your back as a stiff breeze of 4 Beaufort comes in from the sea and messes up the train on the beach.

SPEEDWING

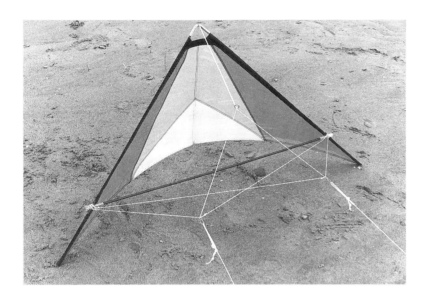

1. The Speedwing is a super fast delta without a central spine.

2. Template with measures in cm, template on cloth.

MATERIAL

0.6 m	spinnaker nylon
2 pcs 1 m	carbon fibre tube 6 mm ∅
1 m	carbon fibre tube 8 mm ∅
8 cm	reinforced vinyl tube 6 mm internal
2 pcs 6 cm	reinforced vinyl tube 8 mm internal
2 cm	vinyl tube 6 mm internal
2.6 m	Dacron band 50 mm width
5 m	bridling line minimal breaking strenght 65 kg
2 pcs	clips breaking strength 75 kg
1 pc	closed aluminum ring
2 pcs	end caps 6 mm internal
	recommended breaking strength control lines: 50 to 80 kg

TEMPLATE

Make a template according to the drawing and outline it on the spinnaker nylon. Mind the grain of the cloth. Side B-C can be cut out just like that but add to the sides A-B and A-C at least 7 mm for a single hem, or 15 mm for a double hem (to be determined by yourself). Cut out two of these pieces of spinnaker cloth.

HEMS

First hem the sides A-C, then put the two wing halves together on A-B. (Some builders prefer another order: they first put the halves together, then hem the trailing edge). Use the flat stitched seam as described in chapter 8 for the central seam.

NOSE

Draw a line squared on the central seam A-B, 5 cm under the top B. Cut away this tip. Stitch a strip of doubled-up Dacron band of 50 mm width over what has now become the top (central drawing in fig. 3). Then melt off the small protruding corners.

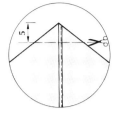

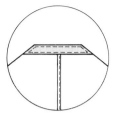

3. Construction of the nose.

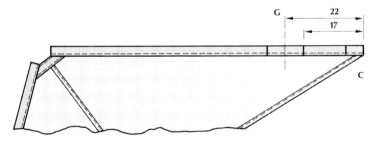

4. Folded back and doubled-up Dacron band. The spinnaker cloth lies inside the wing sleeve, flush with the fold.

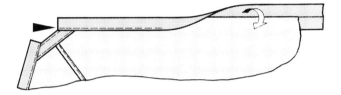

6. The kite after finishing the wing sleeve.

5. The way to start at the nose (cf. black arrow of fig. 4).

WING SLEEVE

1. Cut two pieces of 50 mm Dacron band of 95 cm length each. Fold in the first 20 mm of each strip, then double-up both strips. Stitch the doubled-up Dacron along the sides B-C over the full lengths. Always start at the nose side! Study the picture to see how the doubled-up Dacron is shoved over the cut-off nose of the kite: the nose is placed between the folded-back Dacron band, so that you will be sure of the wing sleeve starting from the correct height. The spinnaker nylon should be shoved up flush with the inside of the fold.
2. Cut off the stitched Dacron band, squared at the points C.
3. Stitch around point C quadruple-folded Dacron band. You have now stitched six layers of Dacron on each other.
4. Stitch a piece of Dacron band (10 cm wide) on each wing sleeve at a distance of 17 cm from C.
5. With a soldering-iron melt a hole G at 22 cm from corner point C in each wing-spar hem. Make a small wooden or metal template for this hole.

NOSE PIECE

The 8 cm long reinforced vinyl tube will become the nose piece. Drill a hole in the middle to

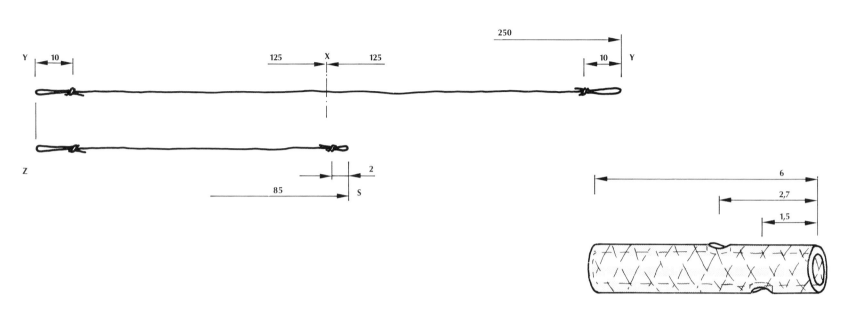

7. The bridle. Top: main bridle, bottom: cross-bridle.

8. The cross fitting is made of reinforced vinyl.

let the bridleline through.

WING SPARS

Saw off the two pieces of the 6 mm carbon fibre at 96 cm. Put them into the hems B-C and shove the nose piece over the ends. When you spread out the kite fully, the Dacron band at top-point C must be taut. In case you cannot spread the kite, shorten the wing spars a couple of millimetres. After these spars have been given the correct lengths, pull them out.

BRIDLE

Prepare a line of 2.5 metres with knotted loops of some 10 cm at both ends. Prepare two lines of 85 cm length each, with a 10 cm loop at side Z and a 2 cm loop at side S.

CROSS FITTINGS

Cut off two pieces of tube of 8 mm internal diameter, each approx. 6 cm long, and drill two 5 mm holes in them, as per fig. 8. These are the cross fittings.

CONSTRUCTION OF FRAME AND BRIDLE

1. Push the long line y-y at its centre x through the hole in the nose piece and thread both ends y through the loop.
2. Cut off four pieces of 6 mm internal tube, 5 mm wide. These rings will prevent the cross fittings from shifting over the wing spars.
3. Make a larks head from the loop and shove it over one wing spar. Then shove a vinyl ring over this wing spar, followed by one cross fitting, another ring and an end cap. Shove the wing spar through hole G to the top B; then wriggle the wing spar through the remaining 20 cm of the wing-spar hem. Repeat this procedure for the other wing half.
4. Attach two clips in the long line with the help of a larks head, at about 35 cm from point G.
5. Attach the loops Z with a larks head to the wing spar at point G and attach them at the other side to the clips.
6. Attach an aluminum ring in the long line y-y at 31 cm from the top B.
7. Cut the ends of the 8 mm spreader at an angle of 45°. Work carefully, for the spreader should keep its length of 1 metre.
8. Put the spreader into the cross fittings. Check the distance between the spreader and point A; it should be approx. 26 cm. If this distance is considerably shorter, the kite sail

9. The kite showing details of nose, spreader and bridle.

10. In order to determine the degree of billowing of the sail, you must measure the distance between spreader and the sail's trailing edge.

will be too taut. In that case you have to push the cross fittings down, i.e. away from the nose of the kite. In case the distance between point A and the spreader is considerably more than 26 cm, the sail will be too slack. The cross fittings must then be shoved towardsthe nose of the kite. When you have attained the correct billowing, glue the vinyl rings (cf. point 2) with a transparent hobby-glue or ultrafast super-glue, so that the cross fittings cannot shift anymore. The kite is now ready.

TIPS

You can make endless variations on the 'Speedwing' theme: a more billowing sail, a longer bridle, spreader attached to the wing spars at another spot, etc. The version described here is a compromise: we wished to build the largest possible kite from 3 times 1 metre carbon fibre, which could take to the air at little wind and would still function well at 5 Beaufort without adaptations. For these reasons the kite has an 8 mm carbon fibre spreader, whilst the wings contain 6 mm carbon fibre. From 6 Beaufort this does not work: the spreader will bend too much and the wing spars will begin to jitter in an annoying way. The solution for this problem is simple: just shove a 10 mm glassfibre tube over the spreader and two pieces of 8 mm glassfibre tube over the wing spars. As regards the length of these reinforcement tubes, the 10 mm glassfibre tube should fit exactly between the cross fittings (approx. 91 cm). After having temporarily removed the nose piece, starting from the nose end, shove 8 mm glassfibre tubes over the 6 mm carbon fibre rods. They should fit between the cross fittings and

the nose piece (approx. 65 cm). An even simpler solution would be to build the kite in a stronger version right from the beginning.

If you shorten the spreader of a Speedwing, or shove the cross fittings down, the sail will billow more. The kite will go up easier but fly slower. With a taut sail the speed is higher but the launching more difficult. However, when you shove the cross fittings down while inserting a longer spreader at the same time (which causes the sail to billow just as much), you will get a faster and firmly steerable Speedwing. The longer spreader in its turn demands more rigidity.

Some more variations: the length of the cross-bridle lines determines the maneuverability of the kite. The longer these lines, the more maneuverable the kite. When it starts jolting while cornering, you have reached the limit.

The place of the central aluminum ring in the bridle determines the relation between cornering behaviour and flying a straight path. If pull on the straights is good, but drops during looping, this central ring should be moved down, away from the nose. Should the kite pull harder in loops, the ring must be shoved upwards. This should be done in combination with a change in bridle adjustment.

The ends of the fibre tubes have a tendency to crush when in a gale the kite is jammed into the ground repeatedly. Glueing small pieces of wood inside the ends of the tubes is certainly of great help to prevent this.

The Speedwing is built sturdier than most other kites of the same size because it has to endure much stronger forces.

TEAM-LIGHT

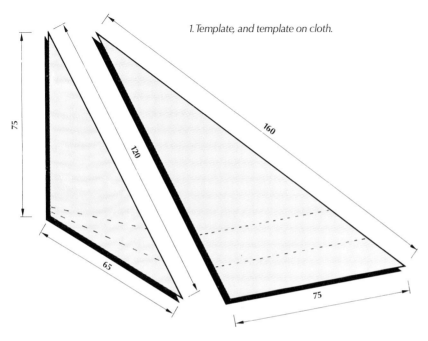

1. Template, and template on cloth.

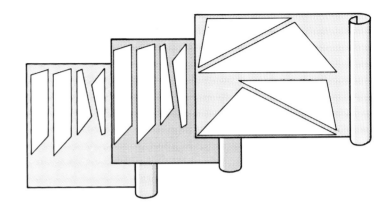

2. The Team-Light is the best team kite for light winds. Note the windbag in the background.

MATERIAL

1.5 m	spinnaker nylon 35 gr/m² main color
0.5 m	spinnaker nylon 35 gr/m² second & third color
4 m	spinnaker nylon 65 gr/m² strip 4 cm wide
7 m	spinnaker nylon 65 gr/m² strip 2 cm wide
2 pcs 165 cm	carbon fibre tube 6 mm Ø
2 pcs 82.5 cm	carbon fibre tube 6 mm Ø
1 pc 150 cm	carbon fibre tube 6 mm Ø
2 pcs 150 cm	carbon fibre tube 3 mm Ø
3 pcs	end caps 6 mm Ø
4 pcs	end caps 3 mm Ø
6 pcs	arrow nocks div.
20 cm	vinyl tube 6 mm internal
10 cm	vinyl tube 4 mm internal
1 pc	stunt kite T-fitting
1 pc	brass connector tube 6 mm Ø
1 m	bungee cord elastic or 50 cm waistband-elastic
5 m	bridle line, breaking strength 80 kg
2 pcs	bridle clips
	recommended breaking strength for control lines: 40 to 65 kg

TEMPLATE

Each wing of the Team-Light consists of at least two large panels, the template measures of which are given here. The trailing-edge can be finished with hemming-band, or by means of a normal folded hem; mind this fact when cutting out the material.

The large surface of this model simply invites the use of multi-color panels. The template shows an example with dotted lines. Then cut the template according to this pattern and put the various parts on the differently colored pieces of cloth. These should be of the lightest possible spinnaker nylon - 35 gr/m² at the utmost - if you wish to preserve the light-wind characteristics. Note the way the various template parts are put on the cloth. Grain squared on the trailing-edge, the larger parts squared on spine and wing sleeve.

The kite was designed *Light*, meaning that the use of heavy Dacron for tunnels and re-inforcement pieces has been avoided as much as possible. Instead of building this model the *Light* way, it can also be constructed as a *Standard* model, with 9 x 7 mm glassfibre for instance, or 8 x 6 mm carbon fibre tubing for the frame. This should be taken into account before stitching. In that case use 6 cm of folded Dacron for the wing sleeves, double-3 cm for the spine tunnel and double-2.5 cm for the sail battens. Reinforce all corners with triangular pieces of Dacron, as described with the Standard-200.

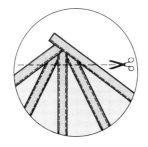

3. Nose.

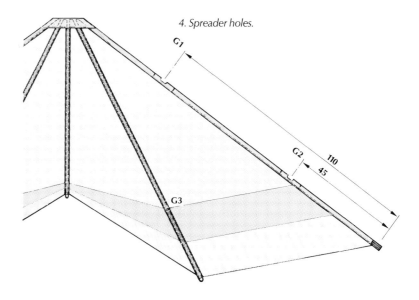

4. Spreader holes.

WINGS

You have to start stitching the various color parts together first, resulting in four large kite parts, two for each wing.

Now hem the trailing-edges first. Then take a strip of 65 gr spinnaker nylon of 2 cm width and draw a pencil-line over the whole length, exactly in the middle. Two wing parts are now glued onto this strip, flush with the pencil-line. At the end of the strip fold a couple of centimetres of the strip back inwards. A second strip is laid over it, after which the whole thing is stitched along both edges with sufficient space in between so that a sail-batten with an end cap can be shoved through it later on.

WING SLEEVES

First double-up the 4 cm wide strips of 65 gr nylon, lay the wing fabric inside the folded strip, flush with the inside of the fold, then stitch it (as with the Standard-200). At the wing tip fold a couple of centimetres inwards as a reinforcement. Reinforcement strips G1 and G2 can now be attached to the places shown.

CENTRAL SEAM

With the help of the 2.5 cm wide strips of 65 gr cloth the two wings are then connected to each other, the spine tunnel to be shaped like the sail-batten tunnels.

FINISH

1. The top is cut on the spot where the strips coincide, and is finished in Kevlar material so as to keep the kite really light. If you cannot get this material, webbing will be indispensable. Dacron fabric appears to wear out too easily.
2. We have chosen to use waist-band elastic for the wing sleeve ends and spine bottom. This material can easily be stitched onto the kite and looks quite nice, instead of the bungee cord plus arrow nock construction. Take strips of 8 cm length, 2 cm wide, double them up, allow the fold to protrude 2 cm and stitch the remaining material along the edges. The elastic will fall inside a broad arrow nock and hence will hardly wear off. We have applied bungee cord to the sail-batten ends.
3. The last thing to do with the sail is to cut - with a soldering-iron - the various holes, G1 and G2 for the spreader attachment, G3 for the tightening struts, called whiskers or stand-offs (cf. Appendix under point 6).

FRAME

The frame measures given are indicative figures which may vary a little with each kite. Even if you are building two identical kites from the same templates, during the stitching the material may shift or stretch somewhat, depending on the kind of nylon used. Therefore be careful when sawing the struts according to the measures given, you had better saw them longer rather than shorter.

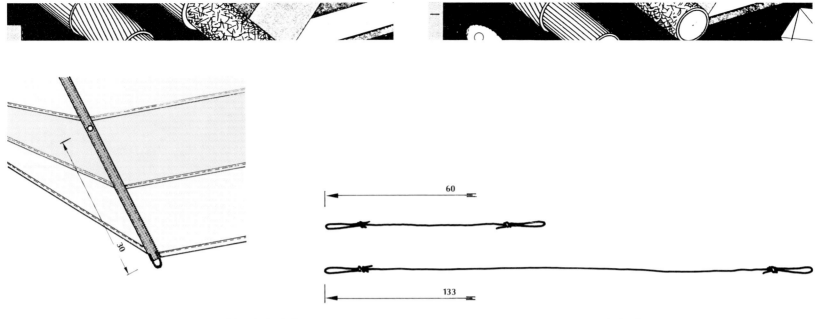

5. Position of the whisker hole.

6. The bridle.

1. Spine of 75 cm 6 mm carbon fibre with end cap at the nose and a nylon T-fitting at the bottom side. Tighten with waistband-elastic sewn on at the same time, or with bungee cord as with a Standard-200.

2. Wing spars 160 cm of 6 mm carbon fibre, end cap on the nose and a special forked end for the waistband elastic.

3. Sail battens 120 cm of 3 mm carbon fibre with end caps and arrow-nock ends glued with two-component glue.

4. Lower spreaders 82.5 cm of 6 mm carbon fibre attached with vinyl tube to wing spars and brass connector in the nylon T-fitting.

5. Top spreader 74 cm of 6 mm carbon fibre attached by vinyls. This top spreader must be secured against shifting along wing spar by glueing a small piece of vinyl right under the joint on the wing spar.

6. Whiskers 21 cm of 3 mm carbon fibre squeezed between lower spreaders and sail battens. An arrow nock clicks exactly on the 3 mm carbon fibre through hole G3. Small rings of vinyl prevent shifting. The connection to the spreaders can also be realized with 4 to 5 mm vinyl tubing (cf. Appendix under point 6).

BRIDLE

The build-up of the bridle is also comparable to that of the Standard-200. First we knot four lines with 10 cm loops at their ends. Two long pieces will be 132 cm long after knotting and are looped around the T-fitting and G1. Attach a clip with a larks head at roughly half the length. Two short pieces of 60 cm run from G2 to the bridle clip.

ADJUSTMENT

The Team-Light is difficult to tune because the proper bridle point is hard to define. When you are used to some other delta stunters, the turning characteristics will be disappointing in the first instance. This might cause you to adjust the bridle too heavily. In that case the light-wind character gets lost while the 6 mm fibre is not fit for the greater forces at such low bridling.

Adjust the bridle in such a manner that the Team-Light will go straight up with just one pull at its lines, even with light wind. Sharp, angular turns should not be a problem. In loops you should steer more carefully, the kite flies in a precarious balance and flutters down uncontrollably after one rash pull at the line. It demands respect from the pilot, but in a team ballet it is the finest kite you can have. With stronger winds the problem will solve itself automatically, but a wind-force of 4 Beaufort is already too much for a 6 mm carbon fibre model.

The Team-Light with its large sail surface is also attractive as a Power Kite. In that case it needs a glassfibre frame of at least 9 mm, or even better: of 8 to 9 mm carbon fibre tubes. With the stronger wind-forces you will then have to deal with, the bridle can be adjusted a bit lower. With wind-forces of 4 to 5 Beaufort, working the control lines will become hard work. Control lines of 135 kg are then a must.

STANDARD-200

1. The Standard-200, most all-round stunt delta.

2. Template with measures, template on cloth.

MATERIAL

3.5 m	Dacron band 5 cm width
1.5 m	Dacron band 2.5 cm width
0.5 m	Dacron band 8 cm width
0.5 m	nylon webbing (seat belt) or Kevlar band 6 cm width
1.5 m	spinnaker nylon
4 pcs 1.5 m	carbon fibre tubes 6 mm ∅
20 cm	thick-gauge vinyl tube of 6 mm internal
3 pcs	end caps of 6 mm
2 pcs	arrow nocks of 6 mm
1 pc	plastic cross connector
7 cm	brass tube 6 mm internal
5 m	bridle line (75 kg)
2 pcs	bridle clips breaking strength 75 kg
1 m	bungee cord
	recommended breaking strength of 50 to 80 kg for the control lines

TEMPLATE

Make a template with the measures given and copy it onto the spinnaker cloth. Mind the grain of the material. The template's measures are already inclusive of the hem for the trailing-edge. So you do not have to draw an extra borderstrip; the nylon can be cut exactly along the template's cardboard edges.

BOTTOM HEM

Cut two triangular pieces of Dacron to reinforce the central corners A. Stitch them on the cloth and hem the bottom side A-C with a double hem, 1 cm wide. The hem overlaps the lower edge of the reinforment pieces. (cf. fig. 3)

WING-SPAR TUNNEL

Double-up the 5 cm Dacron band carefully over its whole length. Then cut off two pieces of 1.5 m each. Now shove side B-C into the Dacron band flush with the fold and glue/pin/staple it temporarily. Stitch the wing spar tunnel at about 3 mm from the edge. Cut off any remnants at the vertexes B. From the remaining piece of 5 cm Dacron cut 6 pieces of about 10 cm length each and stitch them on points G1, G2 and C.

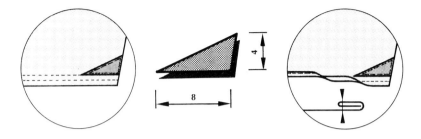

3. The reinforcement piece of Dacron cloth is sewn on the back of the kite. Then hem the bottom edge.

4. The wing-spar tunnel with Dacron reinforcements.

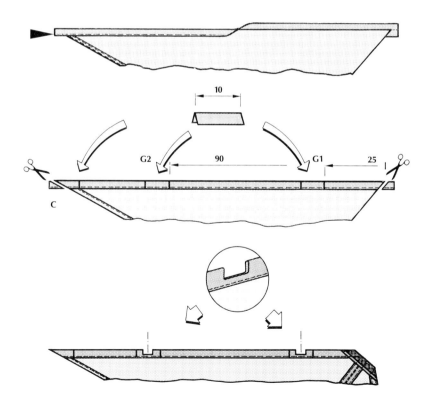

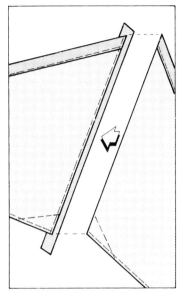

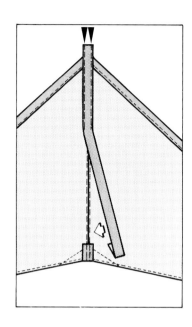

5. The two wing halves are stitched on a Dacron strip. Then a second strip is sewn on the front, thus making up the spine tunnel.

CENTRAL SEAM

Take 75 cm off the 2.5 cm Dacron band. Put side A-B of one wing half exactly on half the width of the Dacron band (advice: glue it). Leave a length of 5 cm of Dacron protruding at the lower end. Stitch the wing to the Dacron at about halfway between the centre line and the edge of the Dacron band. The other wing half is now carefully fitted flush against it, and also stitched. The protruding 5 cm of Dacron is now turned up and stitched. (cf. fig. 5)

SPINE TUNNEL

Of the remaining 75 cm of the 2.5-cm Dacron band turn up 5 centimetres and stitch it over the junction A-B, at about 3 mm off the edge. No glue is necessary for this easy operation. This makes up a tunnel for the spine, whilst the seam is neatly covered up at the same time. If you have worked it out properly, you will see two rows of stitchings at the front of the kite and four at the back.

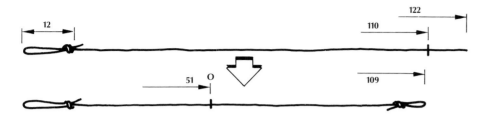

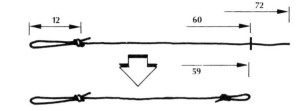

6. The bridle. At the left the main bridle, at the right the side bridle.

7. The nose construction.

8. The holes in the wing-spar and the spine tunnels.

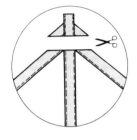
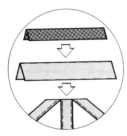

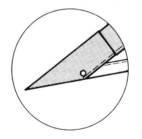
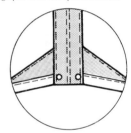

NOSE

Cut off the tip of the nose at the point where the wing-spar Dacron touches the spine Dacron. The 8 cm wide Dacron is placed, doubled-up, over the cut-off nose, to be glued if necessary. Fold the nylon webbing over the nose. In case you use Kevlar band, just forget the remark about the car safety belt. In that case first fold the Kevlar band and then the 8 cm wide Dacron band across the tip. In either case stitch the whole thing according to the drawings. Take care not to stitch up the tunnels. Cut off the remnants obliquely.

SOLDERING IRON

Meanwhile have a soldering iron heated up and melt away all cut-off Dacron edges so as to prevent any fraying. Melt small holes at the vertexes A and C for the bungee cord attachment. Melt four holes of 3 x 1.5 cm at points G1 and G2 in both wing-spar tunnels. It is certainly worth the effort to make a small template for these four holes.

FRAME

1. Saw off a piece of approx. 70 cm from one carbon fibre tube. Put an end cap on one of its ends and the nylon/brass T-shaped connector on the other end. Shove this combination into the spine tunnel and see to it that the nylon T-joint just misses touching the kite sail. If necessary, saw off to measure.
2. For the wing spars saw off two 132-cm pieces of carbon fibre tube. (Before cutting it off, make sure it will fit!) Shove the spar starting from vertex C into the tunnel. Having reached hole G2, place a vinyl stopper, a cross-strut fitting and another stopper on the spar. Keep these three in their respective places and shove the spar further to hole G1. There, fit once again the stoppers and the cross-fitting on the spar, and finally place an end cap on the end of the spar. Shove the spar up to the nose. Fit an arrow nock at the other end of the spar (near vertex C) and stretch a loop of bungee cord across the arrow nock.
3. For the short spreader between the G1 holes, saw off some 40 cm length from the carbon fibre tube of which you had already taken a 70-cm piece for the spine spar. Of the last remaining carbon fibre spar now saw off two pieces of 68 cm each to make up the bottom spreaders. Shove the three spars into their respective places, while seeing to it that the cloth in the upper part is some 3.5 cm free from the spar, and some 14 cm at the bottom spreaders. If necessary, saw them off to measure.

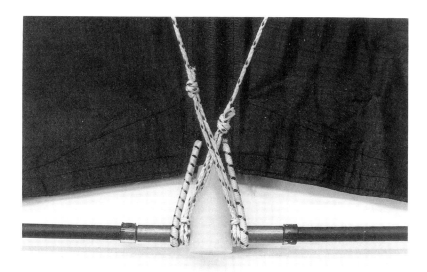

9. The lower part of the spine: T-fitting, bungee cord and the bridle.

10. The wing-spar tunnel with bungee cord stretched across the arrow nock.

BRIDLING

The bridle of the Standard-200 consists of two long and two short lines. As for the long line, set about it as follows: make an overhand knot at the end of the line to tie a 12 cm loop. Measured from the loop, cut off the line at 122 cm and draw some mark at 110 cm. Double-up the unknotted end of the line at the 110-cm mark and knot another loop. Measured from loop to loop the length of the long line must now be 109 cm. Put another mark at 51 cm from G1. First wrap the loops around the carbon fibre/vinyl tube at G1 and then around the T-fitting. Now attach the bridle clip at O.

As for the short line, tie a loop at one end by means of the well-known overhand knot. Put a mark at 60 cm from the loop and cut off at 72 cm. Take the end double on the mark and make an overhand knot. Measured from loop to loop, the short lines should each be 59 cm long. First attach the loops at points G2 and then attach the loose loops to the bridle clips. The kite is now ready and only needs trimming.

TIPS

The bridling of a Standard-200 is less tricky than that of a Speedwing. Between too high bridling (the kite flutters uncontrollably in the air) and too low bridling (the kite cannot be launched), the Standard-200 has a tolerance area of 2 cm in which the kite functions well. If you bridle it high, the kite will climb easily, fly relatively slow and feel slightly slack in the turns, a fine way of flying with very little wind. Bridling the kite somewhere near the lower limit of the trimming, the aggressive Standard-200 becomes evident: hard-pulling, fierce-turning. Launching becomes a problem. Often the combination of a good tug and a few steps backward are necessary to launch it. A compromise between a high and a low trim will take care of flying your kite under almost every condition without further trimming.

Aficionados of a stiff breeze (the safety limit for a carefree flight with a Standard-200 lies around a 5 Beaufort breeze) had better reinforce the spine by pushing an 8 mm glassfibre tube over the 6 mm carbon fibre one, or the spine spar might crack.

You will make a Standard-200 clearly faster by flying it with spreaders that are 1 or 2 cm longer. The kite's sail will become more taut and its pull will increase. It will also be faster in the turns. As against these gains there will be some losses too. It is harder to get the kite going and it will show a tendency to drop dead after tight loops because the wings are being stalled. So for easy-going, concentrated flying (as with team flying) a more billowing sail is to be preferred.

It is quite possible to fly a Standard-200 with four lines, although this will not turn it into a Revolution. Attach a V-shaped line left and right between T-fitting and wing-bridle point. The four lines must be fitted to special grips. You can now stall the kite at any place and in any position. However, it cannot go into reverse. This stalling makes funny tricks possible: stop suddenly while at full speed, fly away and stop again, take off anywhere and land again, make the kite dance up and down with one wing tip touching the ground, and so forth.

KWAT

1. Precarious balance. The four-line Kwat stunter.

2. Template of one of the twelve triangles; templates on the cloth.

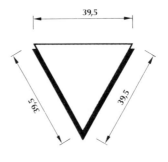

39,5

39,5

39,5

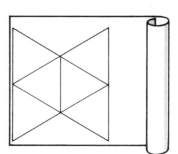

MATERIAL

1.6 m	spinnaker nylon
4 pcs 82.5 cm	carbon fibre tube 6 mm Ø
1.5 m	carbon fibre tube 6 mm Ø
1 m	Dacron or Kevlar band 6 cm width
10 pcs	plastic arrow nocks 6 mm internal
12 m	bridle line breaking strength 50 kg
4 pcs	bridle clips breaking strength 75 kg
2 pcs	vinyl rings, length 5 mm, 6 mm internal
	recommended breaking strength control lines: 20 - 25 kg

TEMPLATE

This kite is built up of two hexagons. Each hexagon consists of six equilateral triangles. This is the only way to realize the possibility to square the grain of the cloth on all outer edges. The template gives the measures of one of those twelve triangles. Outline the twelve triangles on the cloth and add to each edge either 7 mm (for a single hem) or 15 mm (for a double hem). Melt (or cut) out the cloth. Take care that there will remain a strip of 140 cm along the edge of the cloth. The spine tunnel will be made from this strip of cloth.

SAIL

Stitch with a flat-stitch seam six triangles together in such a manner that they will form a regular hexagon. The best way to do this is to first stitch three triangles together (thus forming a half hexagon); then sew the two half-hexagons together, which will result in a whole hexagon. See to it that the grain of the cloth is squared on the outer edges. Hem the edges of the hexagon - after having stitched the triangles together - with a single hem when you have added 7 mm to the basic triangle, or with a double hem in case you have added 15 mm to it. Construct the other hexagon in the same way. Shove the two hexagons 14 cm over each other and stitch them together.

REINFORCEMENT PIECES

Stitch reinforcement pieces of Dacron or Kevlar onto the corners A, B and C at the back of the sail. Consult the drawings for the shape of these reinforcement pieces.

LOOPS

Sew loops onto the corners A, B and C at the back. These loops should protrude some 5 mm outside the sail and should be stitched in such a way that the outer edge of the sail is also sewn with them at the same time. Should you forget to stitch the last part together with them, the sail will eventually curl up when tightening it. These loops are made by doubling-up an 8 x

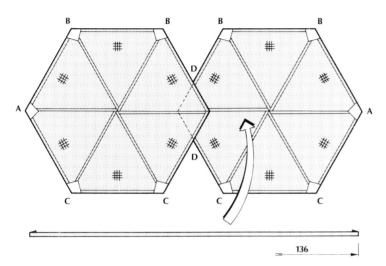

3. The two parts put together. The narrow stip of spinnaker nylon is meant for the cross-strut tunnel.

4. The piece of Dacron or Kevlar of which the loops are made.

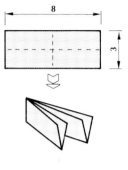

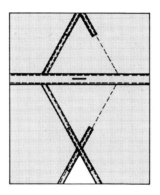

5. The two cross strips in the centre of the kite.

6. The back of the Kwat with tunnel, lace (in this case a strip of spinnaker nylon) and two carbon fibre spars.

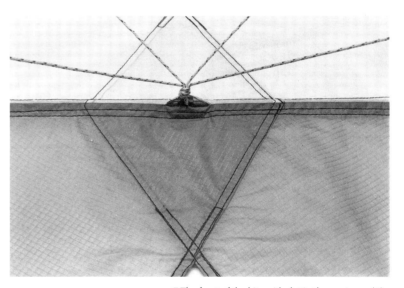

7. The front of the kite with slot in the centre and the four lines of the main bridle.

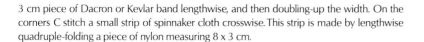

3 cm piece of Dacron or Kevlar band lengthwise, and then doubling-up the width. On the corners C stitch a small strip of spinnaker cloth crosswise. This strip is made by lengthwise quadruple-folding a piece of nylon measuring 8 x 3 cm.

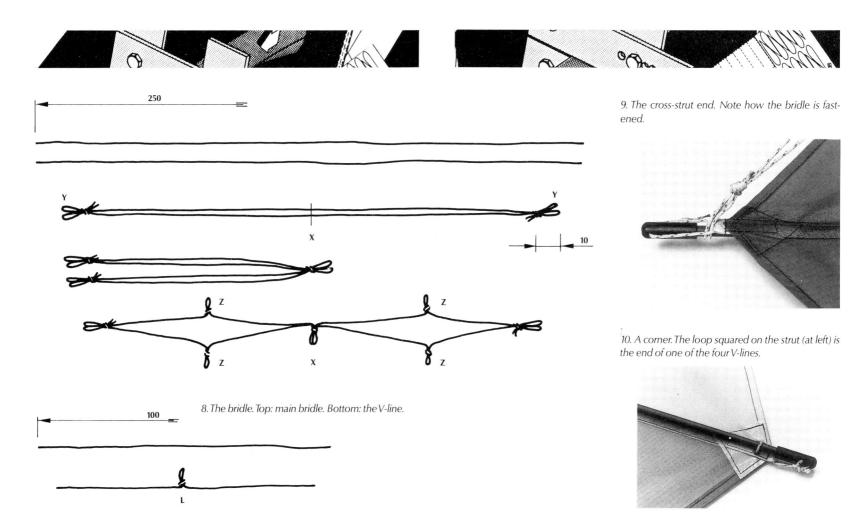

250

Y

Y

X

10

Z

Z

X

Z

Z

8. The bridle. Top: main bridle. Bottom: the V-line.

100

L

*10. A corner. The loop squared on the strut (at left) is
the end of one of the four V-lines.*

CROSS-STRUT SLEEVE

Melt out a strip of spinnaker nylon, 2 cm wide and 140 cm long. At both ends fold-in the last 2
cm. Stitch the strip over the whole width of the kite, at the back, with two seams at 2 mm from the edge. This is going to be the sleeve for the cross-strut. Sew a piece of lace (or something similar) of 30 cm length, squared on the sleeve in the middle of each hexagon. You will
eventually make a bow in this lace, so that the frame will stay in its place. Melt a horizontal
slot of 2.5 cm length in the sleeve and the sail in the centre of the kite.

ARROW NOCKS

Black arrow nocks are placed on the ends of the five carbon fibre tubes. The caps fit tightly
on the carbon fibre. They have a slot at the end to contain the tension-lines. Of the bridle line

cut off ten lengths of roughly 20 cm each, pull them through the ten loops on the sail and tie
overhand knots. Not too tight, as you may eventually have to alter the lengths of the line later
on.

BRIDLE

1. Measure off two lines of 250 cm each. Lay the lines on each other and - by means of an
overhand knot - make two loops of some 5 cm at both ends of the lines taken together.
This will become the main bridle. Grab the centre point X and make an overhand knot in
both lines taken together. You will now have a loop from which four lines of equal lengths
are running, which in turn are knotted together in twos.
2. Shove the 1.5 m carbon fibre cross strut into the sleeve and have it protrude through the
slot in the centre. Shove a vinyl ring over the cross strut, loop X and again a vinyl ring. Shove

11. The Kwat bridle in perspective. The four V-lines are squared on the kite's plane.

12. Everything can be done with a Kwat. Also flying horizontally, with the cross strut parallel to the horizon.

the cross strut further down the remaining part of the sleeve.

3. Lay the loops Y over the two ends of the cross strut, then fasten the end caps on the corners A. The central sleeve should now be really taut. If necessary, shorten the tension lines somewhat.

4. Measure off four lines of 100 cm each. Knot a loop in the centre of all four lines. With a bodkin pierce two holes at all corners B and C, straight through the reinforcement pieces and the loops, at roughly 2 cm from the edge of the sail, and approx. 1 cm apart. Attach the line - by means of a large loop and a slip-knot (cf. chapter 3) - through the holes at B and C, the knot remaining at the front of the kite. Slip the knot in such a manner that the small central loop of the line ends up right in the centre of the kite, at the point where the six triangles coincide. Repeat this procedure of fitting and knotting for the other seven ends of the four top and bottom bridles. When you have done it right, you will ultimately have attached four V-lines to the kite's front, all of the same length and all with a small loop exactly in the centre.

5. Push the four 82.5 cm carbon fibre tubes under the loops of the V-lines and put the end caps over the fibre ends in corners B and C. The nylon cloth should be reasonably slack on the frame. Set right if necessary.

6. Are you still there? Good! Now make four loops by means of an overhand knot in the four lines of the main bridle (cf. point 1 above), the four loops lying exactly opposite the small loops in the top bridles.

7. Measure off four pieces of 30 cm line and knot them at the one side to the four loops L of the four V-lines. At the other side to the four loops Z of the four main lines.

8. Fasten the four clips in the four lines mentioned under point 4 above. Now adjust the clips in such a manner that the four V-lines are exactly squared on the edge of the kite. The kite is now ready for launching.

TIPS

We have not tried it out yet, but we actually think that any flat kite can be converted into a four-line stunter. The only thing you have to take care of is: the kite must consist of two loose parts, and these two parts must be capable of twisting with respect to each other, i.e. turn around the central cross strut. Two squares, two circles, two little hearts, two spectacle glasses, all these will do it, we think, as long as the cloth is not too taut.

We usually fly the Kwat on short lines of 22.5 metres. Thus you can set off with two reels of 45 metres. Spectra is, of course, fine, but not strictly necessary. Dacron will do too. As for the handles, both straight sticks and special quad-handles are used. Either will function alright.

SPEEDFOIL

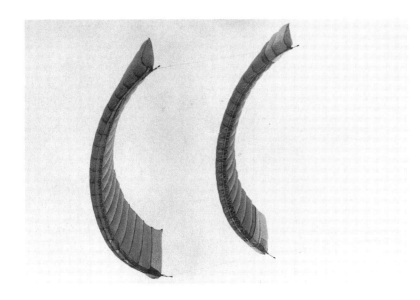

1. The Speedfoil is a superfast cousin of the Flexifoil.

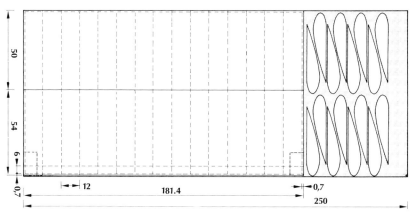

2. The measures of the upper and lower skin.

MATERIAL

2.5 m	spinnaker nylon of 104 cm width
1 set	ULTRA-flex spars up to 5 Beaufort
1 set	standard Flexifoil spars as from 4 Beaufort
1 strip	vitrage gauze 3 x 200 cm
0.5 m	Dacron 8 cm wide
2 pcs	aluminum rings approx. 10 mm with rounded-off edges
0.5 m	seat belt webbing 10 mm wide
	recommended breaking strength of 50-80 kg for control lines

CHOICE OF SPINNAKER NYLON

For this type of kite it is of the utmost importance that the spinnaker nylon fabric is entirely non-permeable to air. The Speedfoil will not fly at all if the fabric lets through the slightest bit of air. The reverse is true for the vitrage gauze: it should be as permeable as possible to air, hence coarsely woven. A second point to pay attention to is the color of the fabric: it is very hard to see where exactly you are stitching with dark colors like black and purple. This applies mainly to the partitions.

How the parts should be cut from the 250 x 104 cm nylon fabric is indicated in fig. 2. As you can see, you will just manage. Both for the upper and the lower skins it is easier to first mark all stitch-lines for the cells at a 12 cm spacing before cutting.

PROFILE

Make two templates for the sixteen profiles: one according to the measures of the index (cf. p. 77, fig. 9) and another one with 7 mm extra material around the edges. Set about it as follows: draw the base-line with the cross lines on the cardboard at the distances indic-

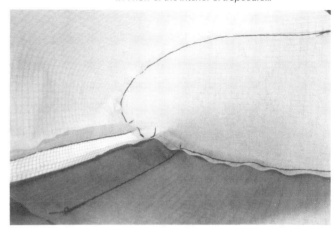

3. The construction of the leading edge corners and the tunnel.
4. A view of the interior of a Speedfoil.

ated. Mark the profile heights on the cross lines according to the index. Now connect the points thus obtained by a smooth, flowing line and cut out. The larger template is easy to make by laying a thick cord around the first template, then outline it and cut.

It is of great importance to mark exactly the gauze/tunnel transition on each profile. It is from this point that you will start sewing in the profiles later on, which procedure should be precisely the same for each profile. Errors of a few millimetres will produce visible distortions in the wing as a whole.

STITCHING

1. **Corner reinforcements.** To start, sew two 8 x 20 cm pieces of Dacron at the leading edge corner of the lower skin. The strongest forces will affect these points of the kite.

2. **Tunnel.** The tunnel or sleeve for the wing spar is shaped by making a crease in the fabric, as it were, and then stitching it flat again. For this purpose take the edge of the lower skin and fold up 37 mm of it, so that the 7 mm line will coincide with the 6 cm line. The 3 cm wide strip of gauze is stitched on the same line. This can be done in one or two stitching-runs. Before finishing the tunnel, its ends must first be finished. Fold up the ends of the two-layer strip at an angle of roughly 45 degrees. Stitch this corner together with the loop of car-belt webbing (10 mm wide and 15 cm long, folded over to a length of 7.5 cm). At the same time sew the aluminum ring in this loop too. Now the tunnel can be flattened and sewn up. Strong finishings of the beginning and the end of this tunnel are very important. To achieve this, stitch up and down a couple of times, shifting the fabric somewhat each time, so as to distribute the forces over a larger area of the fabric.

The upper skin can now be stitched at the other side of the gauze, again at 7 mm from the edge. A 16 mm strip of gauze remains.

3. **Profiles.** Take the partitions and first stitch them all with their top sides to the upper skin. Each time start exactly at the mark on the edge of gauze and tunnel. Take care that the seam is turned inside with the first and the last profile.

Then with the first profile start again from the tunnel edge and stitch the lower skin to the bottom edge of each profile. Always take care to start stitching meticulously, and do not sew up the tunnel fully closed; 3 centimetres of each profile remain unsewn.

4. **The last cell.** It makes no difference whether sewing the profiles is started from the left or from the right of the kite; you always have to fumble with an awkward heap of kite material under the arm of your sewing-machine. The moment will soon be there that you will come to the last profile (there is no escaping it), which makes you wonder, in the first instance, whether the seam can ever be on the inside. Fortunately things are not that bad. The top half is already fixed, just start again at that spot and stitch slowly in the direction of the back edge. In order to achieve this, you will have to gradually cram more and more of the kite into the last cell, which is now automatically being shaped inside out. It may sound impossible, but you will see your way as you go along. At the end of the seam, you simply pull the whole kite out of the last cell.

5. **Final seam.** Now you only have to sew up the trailing edge. This can be done in a straight line connecting all the profile ends. The remaining edge can be folded over twice and stitched, or be cut off with the soldering-iron at 3 mm from the seam, so as to achieve a fine, streamlined finishing.

WING SPARS

A standard *spar* (i.e. the stick running through the tunnel under the nose of a Speedfoil to keep the kite spread) consists of tapered glassfibre parts, 8 mm in the middle and 4 mm at the ends, connected by a thick-gauge brass tube. When you build kites smaller than 1.80 m, the spar as a whole should be thinner; kites larger than 1.80 m are provided with a solid carbon fibre centre-piece.

For light winds ULTRA-flex Spars in various sizes are available in three or more parts. These consist of an ALU-Carbon centre-piece with glassfibre tips.

Do-it-yourself construction of these spars is possible with fishing-rod parts.

TIPS

To plunge into the matter rightaway: we did not break the unofficial world speed record with the Speedfoil as described above. That fastest kite has exactly the same profile, but it is not 1.80 m wide; instead, its width is 2.00 metres. This kite has relatively more partitions as well: one every ten centimetres, whereas the variant described in this book has one partition every twelve centimetres. We chose for this type because it will enable you to fly your Speedfoil with a standard spar. Those of you who truly love high speeds can, of course, build a two-metre wide foil; however, you will have to get hold of a solid piece of carbon fibre.

Because the Speedfoil has no bridle lines, attaching and stacking more Speedfoils is a very easy thing. Each end of a control line is provided with a loop, pulled through the aluminum ring and attached to the *spar* by means of a larks head. The kites comprising a Speedfoil train may even be of different wing spans, e.g. 1.92 m (16 cells) for the front kite, 2.16 m (18 cells) for the centre kite, 2.40 m (20 cells) for the last one. You would be well-advised to provide the control lines with a thicker end in any case, in order to prevent wear at the knots and the aluminum rings.

It does happen sometimes that Speedfoils or Flexifoils start shaking or vibrating when flown. This is caused by a faulty spar rigidity. The phenomenon appears hard to cure with stacked foils but single foils can usually be improved by using a stiffer spar. Flapping of a couple of cells at the foil-tips is another thing, which can easily be taken care of by moving the points of attachment of the lines somewhat to the inside, by moving up the rubber rings a few centimetres. A kite may also start flapping after it has become wet; do not worry, this flapping will disappear within a few minutes.

The Speedfoil requires a style of controlling quite different from what you may have become used to with delta-shaped stunters. It is important to realize that the foil will only fly and become controllable the moment the spar starts curving. Only then will it develop forward speed and pull. Keep the kite in this curvature as much as possible; as from 7 Beaufort this happens automatically. At 2 Beaufort, however, it becomes an art and a matter of feeling. After a while you will be able to feel from the tension in the line when the foil is on the point of suddenly stretching itself straight; at that very moment take a few steps back and send the kite back to the centre where the wind will get a good grip on it again.

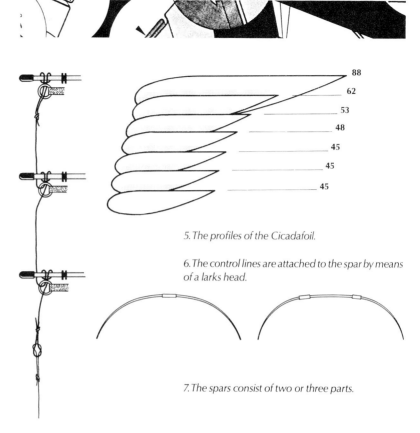

5. The profiles of the Cicadafoil.

6. The control lines are attached to the spar by means of a larks head.

7. The spars consist of two or three parts.

LAUNCHING

To keep such a limp kite in a stand-by position is certainly not easy. Because of the reverse wing profile (flat on top, curved at the underside), a foil will first start flying downwards at its launch, only to streak upwards later on.

– The easiest way is to have an assistant hold the kite over his head. He should only hold the front edge of the foil loosely. Do not forget to explain to your assistant which is the top side of the kite! As soon as the pilot is ready to fly it, the assistant should only let the kite go and not throw it.

– Without any help. Just lay the kite flat on the ground. After a few tugs at the lines the foil will fill itself with air, start bouncing up and down a couple of times, and then fly off all by itself. Actually, things are not quite that easy! On the beach it will merrily fly away before you have reached the handles. On an inland field you may tug and pull as hard as you wish: nothing will happen.

– Launching-sticks. Thrust two glassfibre or wooden sticks of about 1 metre each into the

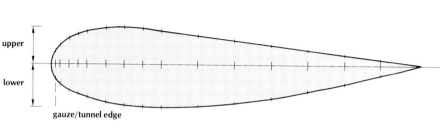

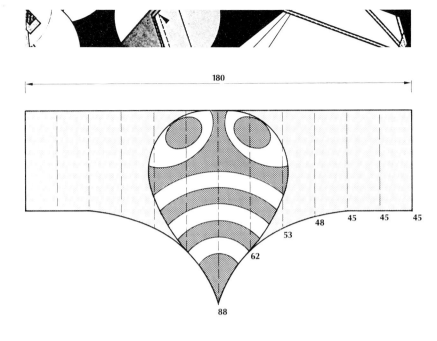

180

48 45 45 45

53

62

88

8. The Cicadafoil is one of the many variants of the Flexifoil.

upper

lower

gauze/tunnel edge

base	upper	lower
6	12	22
11	19	28
23	28	34
34	32	38
45	36	42
68	40	47
90	40	50
113	38	52
135	35	52
180	30	51
225	25	48
270	20	41
315	15	30
360	10	20
405	5	10
450	0	0

9. The wing profile and profile measures for the Speedfoil.

ground, slanting against the wind, and roughly 1.80 m apart.

1. Should you stand on an open field, position the kite behind the sticks. When you pull at the lines, the kite will glide upwards along this 'launching-site', get caught by the wind and fly off.

2. On the beach you should position the kite in front of the sticks, so as to prevent it from going up prematurely. After one tug at the lines the foil will free itself.

3. Both tricks will work, also when several foils have been stacked. Placing launching-sticks for the front and back kite will suffice.

– Should a foil come to crash (even the best pilot can make a mistake), in 99 out of a 100 cases it will come to lie upside down. You can get things right again by simply giving one of the lines a strong tug; that side of the kite will turn round in your direction and slightly beyond, the wind will turn the sail 'downside up' and away it will go again.

SPEEDFOIL HYBRIDS

Tinkering at the design of kites without bridles, such as the Speedfoil, is always a bit risky. If you change too much, the balance may get lost and there is no bridle with which to correct it.

While maintaining the same profile, the width can be changed without any risk. We would advise you to stick to a wing span of at least 1.20 m (10 cells) and not to exceed 3 metres (25

cells). Beyond these limits finding a spar with the correct flexibility/rigidity is rather difficult. Moreover, the following rule is valid: a 1.20 m wing span kite provides the best flight in strong winds, whereas a 3.00 m wing span type gives the best results with moderate wind.

The profile also offers possibilities for experimenting: thickness, length, billowing - all in many combinations - but these are beyond the scope of this book. Deviations from the oblong basic shape of the kite can result in very attractive designs. As an example of the many possibilities, fig. 8 shows the Cicadafoil of the 'Crash' stunt team.

In order to determine the fabric shapes, we have supplied a simple computer programme, worked out in Appendix nr. 7. First think out a design and draw it, taking care that the distances between the profiles are somewhere between 10 and 15 cm. Then measure up the various profile-lengths from your plan. From these lengths the programme will compute the profile data, determining at the same time the whole length around the perimeter, divided between the top and bottom side. Due to the curvature of the profile, the measures of the upper and the lower skin should exceed the profile length. Now add ⅔ of the calculated extra length to the gauze-side and ⅓ to the back edge of both pieces of fabric.

With this method of construction the thickness is proportionally greater at those places where the profile is longer. Because of the curved nose edges the stitching will be more difficult, but the whole of the sewing-procedure remains the same as with the Speedfoil. The Cicadafoil is flown with a standard glassfibre Flexifoil spar.

SPUTNIK 1 & 2

1. Sparless and meant for stronger wind forces: Sputnik 1 (top) & 2.

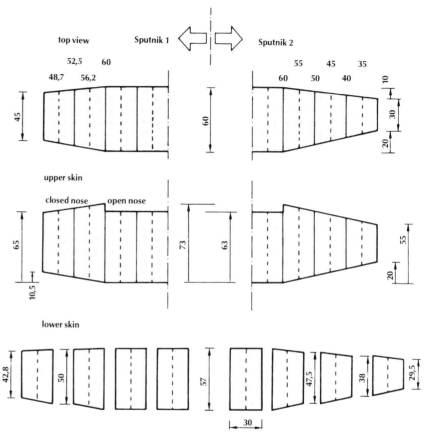

top view   Sputnik 1 ⟵ ⟶ Sputnik 2

upper skin

closed nose   open nose

lower skin

MATERIAL

Sputnik 1	Sputnik 2	
4.5 m	4 m	spinnaker nylon
25 m	15 m	bridle line breaking strength 50 kg
12 m	10 m	Dacron band 2.5 cm width
135 kg	65-90 kg	recommended breaking strength control lines

The tapered wings of these Sputniks require some extra work because they need profiles of different sizes. We would advise you to make a separate template for each profile size, with or without keels.

The most striking aspect about the Sputnik is that only the central cells are open at the front side. This will cause the kite to keep its shape much better during looping. If all the cells are open, the wingtip would lose too much air pressure in the inner curve and the kite would collapse.

To achieve this shape the upper skin should continue, at the tips, beyond the nose until the lower skin. Another important aspect is that the partitions should have holes in them in order to allow the air to flow towards the tips which is necessary for building up air pressure.

CUTTING OUT THE TEMPLATES

The two Sputniks have been drawn side by side: a top view giving the measures after sewing

78

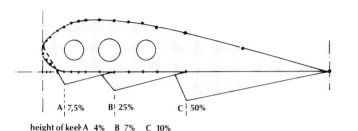

A 7,5% B 25% C 50%

height of keel: A 4% B 7% C 10%

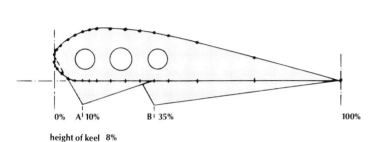

0% A 10% B 35% 100%

height of keel 8%

2. The templates and profiles. At left Sputnik 1, at right 2.

Sputnik 1 profiles

%	600 mm profile			562 mm profile			525 mm profile			487 mm profile			450 mm profile		
0	0	55	38	0	52	36	0	48	33	0	45	31	0	41	29
1,25	8	65	25	7	61	23	7	57	22	6	53	20	6	49	19
2,5	15	73	15	14	68	14	13	64	13	12	59	12	11	55	11
5,0	30	85	4	28	80	4	26	74	4	24	69	3	23	64	3
7,5	45	94	0	42	88	0	39	82	0	37	76	0	34	71	0
10,0	60	100	0	56	94	0	53	88	0	49	81	0	45	75	0
12,5	75	104	0	70	98	0	66	91	0	61	84	0	56	78	0
15,0	90	107	0	84	100	0	79	94	0	73	87	0	68	80	0
20,0	120	109	0	113	102	0	105	95	0	98	89	0	90	82	0
25,0	150	107	0	141	100	0	131	94	0	122	87	0	113	80	0
30,0	180	104	0	169	98	0	158	91	0	146	85	0	135	78	0
35,0	210	99	0	197	93	0	184	87	0	171	80	0	158	74	0
40,0	240	93	0	225	87	0	210	81	0	195	76	0	180	70	0
50,0	300	79	0	281	74	0	263	69	0	244	64	0	225	59	0
70,0	420	48	0	394	45	0	368	42	0	341	36	0	315	36	0
100	600	0	0	562	0	0	525	0	0	487	0	0	450	0	0

up the kite; under this view: the measures for cutting out the upper skin; finally, under that view: the parts comprising the lower skin.

Plot the different profiles according to the measures in the index. Caution: in the centre part the profile-noses are cut off slantingly for the inlet apertures. Secondly, do not make any airflow-holes in the outer profiles. Every other profile is provided with a keel. All measures supplied are stitching-measures; wherever necessary, add 7 mm of extra material for hems and seams.

STITCHING

1. First of all provide the leading edge of the oblong centre part with Dacron band (2.5 cm wide, folded up). This will help to keep open the wind-scooping cells. Also apply Dacron band to the edges of the keels; sew loops at the vertexes to attach the bridle.

Then the parts of the lower skin can be sewn together. Two of those parts are joined together with a profile-plus-keel in the same seam. Take care that the seam-edges are at the inside of the kite.

The tapering wing edge will later on be stitched to the upper skin. Take this into account when sewing on the profiles, hence keep a margin of 7 mm of cloth.

Now the profiles without a keel can be sewn on too.

2. The upper skin can then be stitched along the tapering edges to the tips at the corresponding edges of the lower skin. It is for this reason that the 7 mm margin has been reserved.

Sputnik 2 profiles

%	600 mm profile			550 mm profile			500 mm profile			450 mm profile			400 mm profile			350 mm profile			300 mm profile		
0	0	55	38	0	50	35	0	46	32	0	41	29	0	37	25	0	32	22	0	28	19
1,25	8	65	25	7	56	23	6	54	21	6	49	19	5	43	17	4	38	15	4	33	13
2,5	15	73	15	14	67	14	13	61	13	11	55	11	10	49	10	9	43	9	8	37	8
5,0	30	85	4	28	78	4	25	71	3	23	64	3	20	57	3	18	52	2	15	43	2
7,5	45	94	0	41	86	0	38	78	0	34	71	0	30	63	0	26	55	0	23	47	0
10,0	60	100	0	55	92	0	50	83	0	45	75	0	40	67	0	35	58	0	30	50	0
12,5	75	104	0	69	95	0	63	87	0	56	78	0	50	69	0	44	61	0	38	52	0
15,0	90	107	0	83	98	0	75	89	0	68	80	0	60	71	0	53	62	0	45	54	0
20,0	120	109	0	110	100	0	100	91	0	90	82	0	80	73	0	70	64	0	60	55	0
25,0	150	107	0	138	98	0	125	89	0	113	80	0	100	71	0	88	62	0	75	53	0
30,0	180	104	0	165	95	0	150	87	0	135	78	0	120	69	0	105	61	0	90	52	0
35,0	210	99	0	193	91	0	175	83	0	158	74	0	140	66	0	123	58	0	123	58	0
40,0	240	93	0	220	85	0	200	78	0	180	70	0	160	62	0	140	54	0	120	47	0
50,0	300	79	0	275	72	0	250	66	0	225	59	0	200	53	0	175	46	0	150	40	0
70,0	420	48	0	385	44	0	350	40	0	315	36	0	280	32	0	245	28	0	210	24	0
100	600	0	0	550	0	0	500	0	0	450	0	0	400	0	0	350	0	0	300	0	0

As regards the sewing-work, the closed wingtips are comparable to the Speedfoils: just sew up all the profiles starting from the nose to the back. Having come to the centre part, skip the truncated nose and sew up the rest of the profile from front to back. Also start sewing the very last small profile from the nose, whereby the kite is turned inside out. A good deal of the kite will be situated inside the last cell and can be pulled out again through the back edge. After having checked all the seams once again, finally stitch the back-seam.

BRIDLE OF SPUTNIK 1

1. First connect the keels B and C with V-lines, at a length of 30 cm after having tied the knots.
2. Attach a second V-line to the above V-lines by means of a larks head D, with the same length, and connect to keel A.

3. The bridle adjusting-points E are in this second V-line and are connected to the left or right bridle ring with long lines. Only the central profile is connected to both bridle rings.
4. Adjustment by means of larks head E, and if necessary also with D. Take care that in the air all lines are taut. When the Sputnik does not fill itself with air, or in case it folds double over the whole length of the profiles, move knot E in the direction of the nose. Should the kite easily fill itself and also go up smoothly, but not pull well and fly slowly, move knot E away from the nose.

BRIDLE OF SPUTNIK 2

We have called this bridle, which might look peculiar to parafoil-experts, an arc-bridle. It somewhat resembles a suspension-bridge with the main cable hanging down from two points of suspension and being loaded by tension-lines of different lengths.

3. Sewing the Sputniks is complicated. The picture shows a wing of which the profiles have already been sewn to the lower skin.

4. The bridles. Sputnik 2 has a so-called arc-bridle.

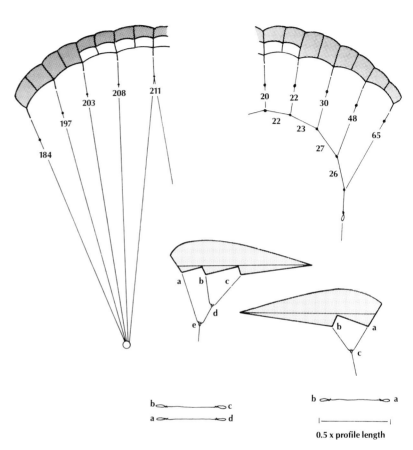

0.5 x profile length

1. The bridle line from keel A to B measures half the profile-length after attaching, hence 30 cm at the central profile and only 15 cm at the outer profiles.

2. Then attach the connecting-lines which - before tying - should be 15 cm longer than indicated, by means of larks heads to these adjustment-bridles (knot C).

3. Now prepare the main bridle line with overhand knots at the intervals indicated.

4. Make a loop in the loose ends of the connecting-lines by means of a slip knot. Then tie all the connecting-lines to the main line by means of a larks head behind each corresponding knot. You can now give these connecting-lines the exact lengths as indicated by making the larks heads larger or smaller with the help of the slip knots.

5. Only larks head C is of importance with regard to the bridle adjustment. Sometimes it is hard to determine which side of the bridle must be adjusted in order to make Sputnik 2 fly at its best. Start at point C, halfway between A and B, then experiment with small changes.

TIPS

Sputnik 1 is an ideal kite to be enlarged and used as a 'wind-engine'. Small carts, boats, skis and the like can be pulled by it at great speed; for this purpose enlarging it by 50 percent to 3.6 meters wingspan is a good option. Yet this kite can be folded and reduced to a small parcel to be taken along. It goes without saying that many derivatives of this model are conceivable. We have seen models shaped as little planes, Dracula, flying reptiles. For the calculation of the profile sizes the computer programme of Appendix 7 can be used.

Sputnik 2 is the best team kite we know for strong winds. Flexifoils and most stunting deltas are too noisy and/or breakable, but Sputnik 2 remains excellently controllable even in a gale, and its pull within all bounds.

GIZMO / CICADA

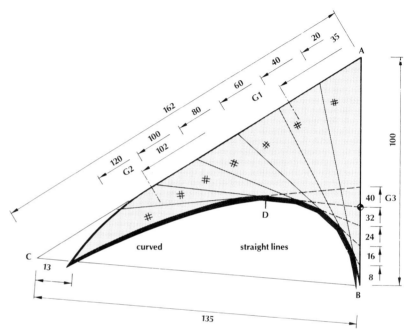

1. The Gizmo is particularly suited to team flying.

MATERIAL

Gizmo	Cicada	
7 x 20 cm	2.3 m	spinnaker nylon 32 gr/m^2
4 m	4.5 m	Dacron band 5 cm width
2 m	2.5 m	Dacron band 2.5 cm width
0.5 m	0.5 m	Dacron band 8 cm width
0.5 m	0.5 m	seat belt webbing or Kevlarband 5 cm width
4 pcs 1.5 m	4 pcs 1.65 m	carbon fibre tube 6 mm ∅
25 cm	25 cm	vinyl tube 6 mm internal
3 pcs	3 pcs	end caps 6 mm ∅
3 pcs	3 pcs	arrow nocks 6 mm ∅
1 m	1 m	bungee cord 3 mm thickness
6 cm	6 cm	brass connector tube
5 m	6 m	braided Dacron bridle line 80 kg breaking strength
2 pcs	2 pcs	bridle clips 75 kg breaking strength
50 cm	50 cm	carbon fibre 3 mm ∅

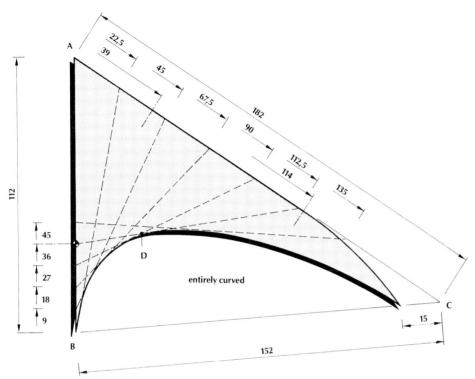

2. The templates for the Gitzmo (left) and the Cicada (right).

2 pcs	2 pcs	mini arrow-nocks suitable for 3 mm
2 pcs	2 pcs	end caps 3 mm ∅
65 kg	90 kg	recommended breaking strength control-lines

In the following text we shall start out from the Gizmo measurements. Wherever necessary, replace them by the figures valid for the larger Cicada.

TEMPLATE

1. Plot the measures for one wing on cardboard. Start with the spine AB, 100 cm. Then plot the oblique side AC at 162 cm and the basic line BC at 135 cm. From G2 (point to attach the lower spreader) the wing side runs curved to the wing tip at 13 cm from C on the base line. Plot this curvature by holding a piece of fibreglass along the oblique side and at the tip bend it inwards. This way you will get the greatest curvature at G2, as required.

2. Now plot the curvature of the trailing edge. Starting from the bottom, mark segments at 8 cm intervals along the spine, and mark 20 cm interval segments along the oblique side, starting from the nose. Then connect these segments by straight lines, each time moving up one box.

3. The trailing edge from B to the wing tip now consists of seven pieces of straight line. You can turn them into a flowing curve when you cut the wing out of one piece of spinnaker; use a 0.5 cm single-folded hem, for a narrow hem simplifies curved sewing work. However, this method is not the economical way, as you will need 1.75 m of spinnaker nylon (2.3 metres for the Cicada) without being able to pay due attention to the grain of the fabric. It is more economical and much nicer to see when you build up each wing from seven small panels, of which the bottom hems can remain straight, with the exception of the seventh panel at the tip. This straight piece of fabric is too long and may easily start flapping; a slight curve here is advisable. As the team photographs in this book show, other patterns are also possible.

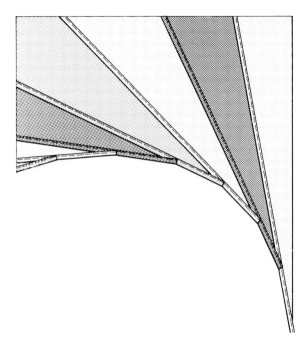

3. The hem of a Gizmo consists of interlocking flat-stitch seams.

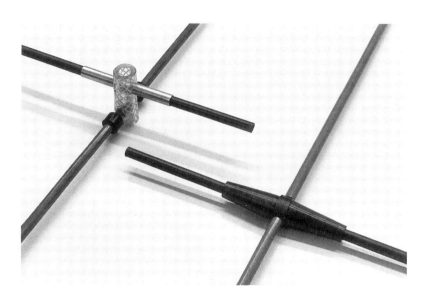

4. The Gizmo cross-fitting. At left a common cross-fitting, at right a lightweight plastic one made on a lathe.

WING

Cut out each wing-panel with the grain squared on the trailing edge of that panel, with 7 mm extra at each side for the connecting seam. On stitching the panels together use a single flat-stitch seam, laid flat in the direction of the spine, so that the bottom hem is sewn in one run. In order to achieve this, first sew all panels to each other with a single seam, stitching from the wing edge towards the trailing edge. After having finished this stage, flat-stitch all seams.

SAIL

The method and the working-order for the construction do not differ from those for the Standard-200:

1. Sew on the wing-Dacron; the curve of the wing tip is laid straight into the Dacron. This may look like resulting in a badly creased wing, but it will appear to be in perfect shape later on when the kite is flown under wind pressure.
2. Reinforcement Dacron at G1, G2 and wing tip.

3. The central seam with spine tunnel between two layers of 2.5 cm Dacron band.
4. Cut off the nose and finish it with Kevlar band or seat belt webbing as well 8 cm Dacron band.
5. Small pieces of Dacron band to be folded round the lower hem at D, to be fixed by small stitches. Melt a small hole in it to attach the whisker (cf. Appendix 6).
6. Melt the holes with the help of a small template at G1, G2 and G3. Melt tiny holes at bottom B of spine and wing tips, to attach the bungee cord.

FRAME

1. First saw off the spine from a piece of 6 mm carbon fibre rod; the remaining part will be needed later for the top spreader. Put an end cap on the top. The joint with the lower spreader is situated at G3. The fitting consists of 2 cm of vinyl squared on the spine, with a brass connector tube again squared on spine and vinyl.
2. Shove a length of 150 cm of 6 mm carbon fibre tube into each wing sleeve. Vinyl connectors of 3 cm length at the apertures G1 and G2 to attach the cross spars.

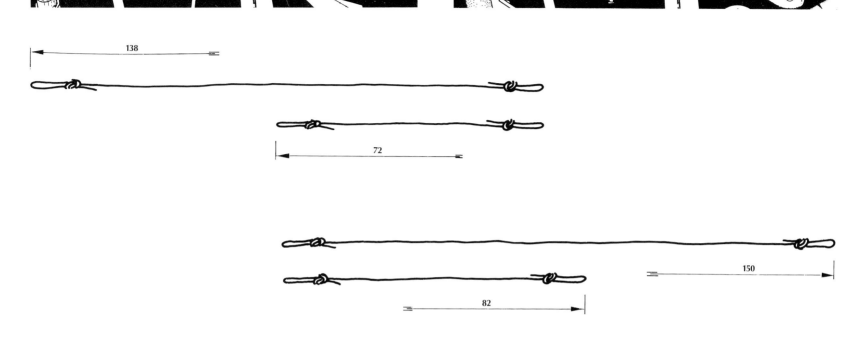

5. The bridles, top: Gizmo, bottom: Cicada.

Underneath G1 an extra ring of vinyl is necessary to prevent the top spreader from shifting. The forces acting on the lower spreader are balanced, so it will remain steady in its place by itself. A few more centimetres may be sawn off the wing spars, the protruding part should be kept as short as possible before the arrow nock is glued on and the bungee cord tied.

3. The lower cross-spars are 75 cm long. When you have sewn the kite properly, small sticks of at least 15 cm length can be squeezed between the sail's trailing edge and the spreader. Attach them with vinyl to the spreader and with a glued, small arrow nock into the hole at D, already melted in the Dacron band. A provision to prevent you from losing this whisker, is a rubber end cap through which you thread a string with a strong needle, to be stitched to the sail at D. The whisker can be held permanently inside this cap by applying some super-glue. The idea is to get the sail's trailing edge taut as a whole. Lengthen the whiskers somewhat or shove the spreaders slightly upwards. Should the sail have become a little too tight after sewing, the spreaders may be sawn off a bit. It is important that 15 cm of sail-billowing is achieved.

BRIDLE

The bridle consists of a piece of line, left and right, of 138 cm length between the loops' ends (hence before attaching to the kite), running from G1 to G3. Fix a bridle clip in this line in such a manner that - when laying the bridle flat on the kite - the clip lies on the spreader. Between this clip and G2 there will be a line of 72 cm between the loops' ends (measured before attaching).

TIPS

With the Gizmo or the Cicada you possess the ultimate acrobatic kite. A fibreglass frame is not at all to be considered for this kite; a good but expensive improvement would be the use of superior alu/carbon tubing by Easton.

The only advice we can give you is: go for it! Do not fly your Gizmo drowsily to and fro, but make it go vividly, balancing it with one wing tip touching the ground, or have it hanging still on one spot. In short, make your Gizmo/Cicada perform a superb aerial ballet!

DYKEHOPPER

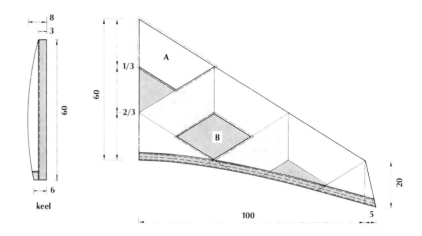

1. The Dykehopper is the only stunt delta in this book with a (profiled) small keel.
2. Template with measures.

MATERIAL

1 m	spinnaker nylon	
	(or 3 x 0.5 m of different colors)	
2 pcs 1 m	RCF 8 mm ∅	
	for the lower spreaders of 94 cm	
2 pcs 1.5 m	RCF 8 mm ∅	
	115 cm in the wings, 30 cm after the notch	
125 cm	RCF 8 mm ∅	
	62.5 cm for the spine, 62.5 cm for the upper spreader	
5 m	Dacron band 6 cm width	
0.5 m	Kevlar band 6 cm width	
1 m	bungee cord 4 mm, or elastic waistband	
0.5 m	reinforced vinyl tube 8 mm internal	
2 pcs 12 cm	8 mm ∅ hardened aluminum tube 1 mm wall-gauge	
1 pc	brass or aluminum connector tube 8 mm ∅	
5 pcs	various end caps, arrow nocks	
	90-135 kg breaking strength control lines	

TEMPLATE

The Dykehopper's shape and its graphic pattern are actually inseparable elements. That is why the measures and the templates are very simple. You only have to make two templates. In order to construct these very accurately, you have to line out the whole wing according to the measures given. Then draw the pattern-lines in it and cut out the two parts A and B with 7 mm extra hemming space around. Cut out shape A in color 1 seven times (e.g. yellow) and again seven times in color 2 (red, for example). Shape B is only needed four times plus two half-shapes at each side of the spine. Two small wingtips and the keel will remain; allow a 7 mm stitching-edge for these parts too.

STITCHING THE SAIL

The sewing of the colored panels can be done with an ordinary flat-stitch seam, although you would have to cheat somewhat at the corners where three colors will coincide at 120° angles. Sew an extra triangle of Dacron or nylon at the nose-corners of both wings, so as to prevent tearing of the nose.

The trailing edge of this kite is not hemmed but provided with a 3 cm wide border of black spinnaker nylon, glued with so-called contact-glue (glue applied to both surfaces to be pressed together after some drying-time has elapsed, at a firm pressure). Then stitch three times.

WING SPARS

So as not to spoil the graphic pattern, the Dacron wing tunnel is stitched with only 1 cm overlap (with other kites the spinnaker fabric is usually laid flush with the fold). In the first 5 cm also sew in a piece of Kevlar band at the same time. It is worth considering to apply Kevlar reinforcements around the spreader holes too. The Dykehopper certainly stresses all material used to the extreme.

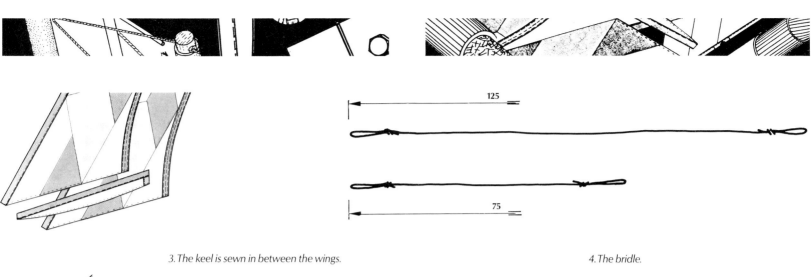

3. The keel is sewn in between the wings.

4. The bridle.

5. Construction of the nose.

KEEL

1. Having finished the wings, reinforce the keel with Dacron along the short back end. Stitch doubled-up 6 cm Dacron band along the long straight side creating the spine tunnel; here too stitch a piece of Kevlar band at the nose side.
2. Wings and keel are sewn together with one seam. Do not be surprised: the wings are straight, while the keel is curved. But this is the way to stitch them together in order to get a fine billowing in the sail later on.
3. Now is the time for the rather special nose construction. Fold the two Dacron wing sleeves flat against the spine tunnel. Force the three Dacron elements in such a manner that their folds will lie on each other (cf. fig. 5). As from now it is merely a matter of stitching them up. Do this with extra strong, thick yarn with a thick needle and small-stitch setting on your machine.

FRAME

The carbon fibre frame now remains to be constructed to measure. The corners at the wing-tips are formed by aluminum tubes bent in the right position. Take care that the material will not buckle while bending it (bending over a block helps) because it would then lose much of its rigidity and would bend during flying. The cross-spars will connect to the wing spar right where the alu-tubes end. The top spreader hooks up ⅓ from the nose.

Finishing the Dykehopper will meet with few problems, just deal with this kite as with a (too) tautly built Standard-200, with the following bridle-line measures: the long bridle lines are 125 cm, loops included, the short bridle lines, including the loops, are 75 cm. For this purpose use lines of at least 80 kg breaking strength.

TIPS

Such a tautly stretched, wide kite is difficult to launch, especially with a moderate wind of 2 to 4 Beaufort. A patient launching-assistant does come in handy, but once it gains speed, the Dykehopper is quite willing to fly at that wind-force. 4 to 5 Beaufort is ideal to adjust the kite, but launching remains a difficult affair, the kite always hesitates a moment or two before actually flying off. Only apply extremely sensitive steering commands, especially for launching, or the kite might otherwise irrevocably crash down again.

If the Dykehopper does not fly well, you should realize that it is very sensitive to 'foul' wind, i.e. to turbulence. Even with the most ideal adjustment, it may not even fly with a 4 Beaufort land-wind that might feel quite nice to you.

A wrong notch in the wing may pose another problem; just experiment with slightly more, or less, bending the wingtip.

The greatest fun with the Dykehopper is in wind-forces exceeding 6 Beaufort, for then the kite will drag you along while at the same time the steering remains extremely accurate and thorough at only small steering commands - square cornering or elegant looping, e.g.

An extra line is visible in the pictures, halfway between the upper bridle lines. This gives the kite even more radical steering characteristics, while reducing oversteer.

APPENDICES

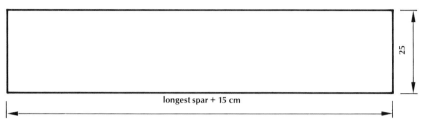

1. Measures of the universal kite sack.

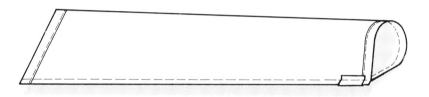

2. The sack inside out.

1 KITE SACK

When your kites are ready, you still have to make a sack. Such a covering will prevent the bridles from getting into one big knot, the whiskers from getting lost and the spars from being mixed up. Making a sack works as follows:

Outline a rectangle on a piece of nylon. For the length of the rectangle take the longest spar of the kite concerned and add 15 cm to it. The width of the rectangle is about 25 cm. Lay the rectangle flat down before you. At the narrow side of the rectangle fold back 3 cm of the nylon fabric and stitch it. This will be the bottom of the sack. At the other narrow side of the rectangle fold back 2 cm; stitch that one too. This will be the open side of the sack. Now double up the rectangle over the whole length, with the stitched edges turned outwards. The sack is still in an inside-out stage. Sew up the long sides, which are put on top of each other and coincide along their lengths, with a seam running approx. 5 mm from the edge. Start from the open side of the sack and at the same time sew also a piece of fabric right at the beginning of this seam, which should prevent tearing of the beginning of the seam later on. Having arrived at the other end, stitch up the bottom too. Now pull the sack inside out, all seams are now invisible at the inside. Pull a string with the help of a safety pin, or something else, through the hem at the open side of the sack and tie a knot in it. Better still: attach a slip-fastening such as you may find in the hood-cord of many rain-jackets, to this string. This way you can fully close the opening of your kite sack by pulling at the string. Another tip: choose the same color of nylon as the one for the kite. This will simplify finding the right kite on the flying-site.

1. The bag in use.

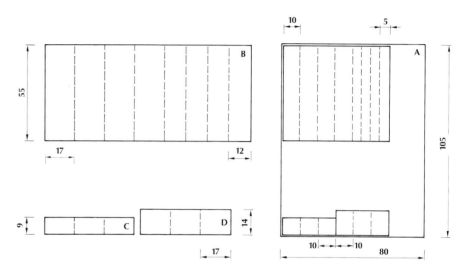

2. The bags measurements.

2 TRANSPORTATION BAG

Several kites are transported together in one large bag, preferably made of some strong material. We designed a kite bag which is simple to make - you don't have to insert long zippers - and, at the same time, provides a handy survey of the kites taken along.

The measures of the bag are such that the kites can be transported the compact way: with the larger models you first have to divide the wing spars, Flexifoils and Speedwings can be easily put in without much ado. The bag's volume adapts itself to the number of kites contained. The nice thing about these bags is that they can always be tightened to size.

Should the majority of your kites be longer than 1 metre or without divisible wings, just make your bag deeper, 150 or 125 cm instead of 105 cm. In that case change the measures of cloths A and B, but do not make C and D deeper than indicated.

MATERIAL

The bag is made of canopy-cloth or of heavy tent-canvas. This material is coated or impregnated, so that the bag is quite water-repellent. It also feels nice to the touch, will wear well and gives the right toughness to the bag, providing good protection for the kites.

CUTTING OUT

You do not have to make a template first; parts A, B, C and D can easily be drawn on the canvas with a soft pencil.

These types of cloth will easily fray yet cutting them out with a soldering-iron is impossible. That is why we have piped all the edges with band after cutting. Hemming is also possible of course. In the latter case you will have to add an extra 2 cm all round the four parts when lining them out. Caution: not all sewing-machines will be able to stitch through four layers of thick canvas which have meanwhile developed at the vertexes.

STITCHING

Parts B, C and D are stitched onto part A. First along the crease-seams of the bag, lengthwise, as indicated by the dotted lines. The intermediate distances on part A are narrower than on the other parts, constituting the tunnels for the kites. Sew up these tunnels at the top sides of C and D and at the bottom of B. The extra cloth is folded back and then flat-stitched.

FASTENINGS

The bag is pulled to close by means of two tension-strips of 50 cm length and 30 mm width, stitched to the outside of piece A. Sew them on with a kind of cross-pattern, as indicated, leaving some space to eventually attach a shoulder-strap.

Pulling to close it can be done with two buckles, but two quick-snaps cannibalized from an old suitcase, for example, are certainly much handier.

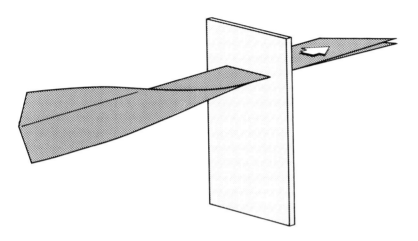

1. The simple folding device: a wooden plank with a slot.

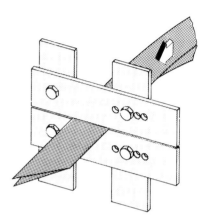

2. Adjustable and practically wearproof: the metal folding device.

3 FOLDING DEVICE

The wing hems of stunt deltas are mostly made of Dacron band. The strip should first be doubled-up lengthwise. Easy enough for one single kite, but for a whole series of kites it is advisable to construct a strip-folding device first. It doubles up the band exactly along the centre line like a razor-edge.

We designed two types: a simple one and an adjustable type. The latter is more durable and adjustable for each band-width. First the simple type.

Take a wooden plank (plywood of at least 6 mm thickness) or an aluminum plate (at least 3 mm thick). Mark it with a pencil line with a length of half the width of the band: for instance, if the band is 5 cm wide, the pencil line should be 2.5 cm long. Drill a hole of 1 to 1.5 mm in the centre of the line and use a fret-saw to saw a slot running from one end of your pencil line to the other. Work accurately!

Fasten the plank in a bench-vice or to a table with a cramp. Double up the first five centimetres of the band by hand, with a pair of scissors cut it into a sharp point. Do it in such a manner that you will cut away the fold itself, leaving you two loose points. Push these two points through the slot. Grab the piece of band at the other side of the plank and pull it through in one steady motion. Within a couple of seconds you will have 10 metres of doubled up hemming-band ready to use.

You might make a separate slot in the wood for each type of band-width. After a while the slot will be worn out and you will have to saw out a new slot.

The less simple device consists of four metal strips of at least 3 mm thickness, about 3 cm wide and 10 cm long. Lay down two parallel strips with half a millimetre spacing between them. Squared on these two strips fasten the other two strips with bolts and nuts. By drilling holes in the first pair of strips at 5 mm intervals, you can fasten the squared strips at every relative distance, thus making it suitable for each conceivable width of Dacron band. Additional advantage: this device is practically wearproof.

Finally, pay due attention to the position of the Dacron band in relation to the slot of the device. Study the drawings.

1. The foam grips are stuck onto a fork.

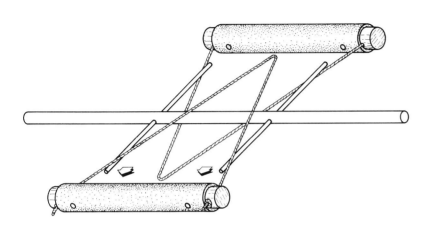

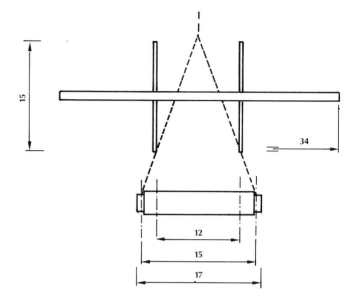

4 FOAM GRIPS

You can easily make these comfortable grips yourself. For the core of the grips, use 22 mm ∅ dowel. A broomstick, for example. Saw off two lengths of 17 cm. Drill a 3 mm ∅ hole at 1 cm from both ends. At 2.5 cm from both sides drill a 5 mm ∅ hole to contain the small 'fork' with which your two flying lines can be rolled up in one movement. Shove a 15 cm long foamrubber tube, as used to cover the handlebars of a bike, over the grip, and glue it. Now thread a 60 cm long line (preferably 135 kg Skybond or stronger) through the two outer holes and tie them with an overhand knot. This V-line is attached to the control line with a larks head.

For the fork use a small piece of dowel, 34 cm long, 12 mm ∅ . Squared on this spar drill two 4 mm holes with 12 cm spacing. For a proper fit of the handles onto the fork, all the holes in the fork and handles need to be drilled very accurately and squared in the same plane. Glue two pieces of 4 mm fibreglass of 15 cm length in these two holes.

After flying your kite, stick the two grips on the fork and take in your lines, rolling them transversely to the grips. The fork is pushed through the foamrubber tube (first pierce them with a pricker).

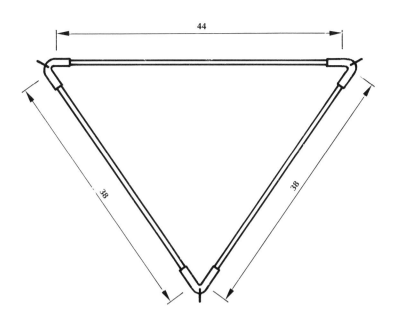

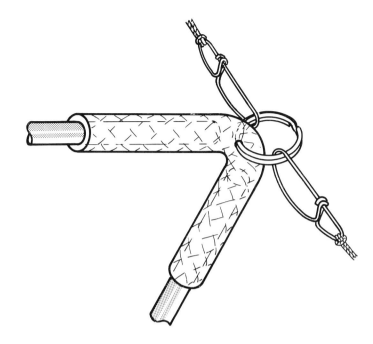

5 TRIANGLE

1. The triangle prevents the first kite of a train from being crushed.

A simple carbon fibre triangle can prevent the front kite of your Shuttle train from being crushed. Saw off three pieces of 6 mm carbon fibre tube as indicated in the drawing. Cut off three pieces of reinforced vinyl tube, of 6 mm ∅ internal and 8 cm long. Pierce holes in the tube at 2 cm intervals and thread a large key-ring through the holes with the help of a pair of tongs. Shove the three pieces of carbon fibre tubes into the three lengths of vinyl tube. With three lines of equal lengths, and with clips, attach the front Shuttle to the rings at the triangle's vertexes. At the other side of the triangle attach the bridle with clips to the three vertexes.

The large key-rings can stand a 40 kg breaking strength. If you expect even stronger forces on the triangle, do not attach the clips to the rings, but to each other. The forces will then be transfered to the clips and the triangle will help retain the shape of the first kite.

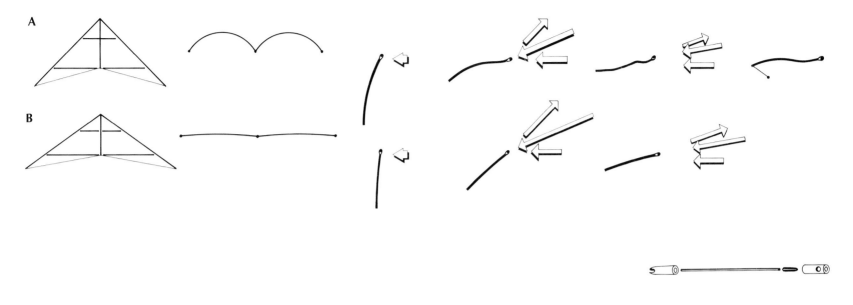

6 WHISKERS

1. A whisker is squared on the lower spreader and pushes the kite's trailing edge taut. The arrow nock fits onto a piece of string sewn in the trailing-edge hem. A cap is put on the other end of the piece of fibreglass. This cap, in its turn, is shoved into a piece of vinyl.

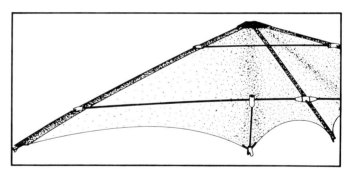

Many modern stunt deltas are supplied with whiskers. These are short pieces of fibreglass or carbon fibre, squeezed between frame and sail to keep the sail taut. The idea behind this is the following:

Kites with a very billowing sail will go up easier than kites with a taut sail. We shall try to explain this phenomenon with the following sketches.

Identical kites, A with a billowing sail, B with a taut one.

Sail A has a smooth flow, sail B an abrupt flow. As soon as the kites are at speed, counter-billowing will become apparent in sail A, as with a sailing-boat on a windward course, of which the mainsail has not been tightened sufficiently. Kite B retains its shape better and

therefore flies faster. In the case of sail A there is a chance of the counter-billowing becoming too extreme, resulting in the sail to luff. At that moment the kite will come fluttering down, out of control.

A whisker towards the sail's trailing edge can postpone the luffing as long as possible. If it should happen anyway, the chances of spontaneous correction are much greater.

Whiskers also take care of re-launching a kite which has landed flat on its back without any help from others.

Finally, kites with whiskers usually make much less noise than kites with unsupported sails.

	A	B	C	D	E	F	G	H
1	base	coordinates		base	coordinates		perimeter	
2	measure	upper skin	lower skin	measure	upper skin	lower skin	upper skin	lower skin
3	450			620				
4				1.0				
5	6	12	22	8	17	30	0	0
6	11	19	28	15	26	39	12	11
7	23	28	34	32	39	47	33	29
8	34	32	38	47	44	52	49	45
9	45	36	42	62	50	58	65	62
10	68	40	47	94	55	65	97	94
11	90	40	50	124	55	69	127	125
12	113	38	52	156	52	72	159	156
13	135	35	52	186	48	72	190	187
14	180	30	51	248	41	70	252	249
15	225	25	47	310	34	65	314	311
16	270	20	40	372	28	55	377	374
17	315	15	31	434	21	43	439	437
18	360	10	21	496	14	29	502	500
19	405	5	10	558	7	15	564	564
20	450	0	0	620	0	0	626	628

7 COMPUTER PROGRAM

This program is meant for those of you who want to design variations of Sputnik and Speed-foil (like the Cicadafoil) themselves. It can also be used for other kite models with wing profiles. A wing profile as a whole can be enlarged or made smaller by multiplication of both the height-measures and the intervals on the base line by the same factor. For example, if you wish to enlarge a profile of 50 cm length and 12 cm thickness by factor 1.5, it will become 75 cm long and 18 cm thick.

The program will do all the computing for you, including the total outline (perimeter) of the profile, so that at each point of the perimeter of the profile it will be clear how much fabric is needed for both the upper and lower skins. You have to keep an eye on gauze and tunnel yourself.

It is also possible to use a distortion-factor, i.e. a factor larger or smaller than factor 1, to produce thicker or thinner profiles respectively.

In order to utilize this program, a simple computer (PC) is necessary. The programming data given below can be entered into most spreadsheets.

The profile data known are entered into columns A, B and C. Columns D, E and F give the corresponding computed data. Columns G and H show the data for the perimeters, of which the bottom-figure is mainly used.

Programming data

A3	=	base profile length
D3	=	profile length desired
D4	=	distortion-factor
D5 to D25	=	([D3]/[A3])*A5
E5 to E25	=	[D4]*([D3]/[A3])*B5
F5 to F25	=	[D4]*([D3]/[A3])*C5
G6 to G25	=	SQUARE ROOT((D6-D5)^2+(E6-E5)^2)+G5
H6 to H25	=	SQUARE ROOT((D6-D5)^2+(F6-F5)^2)+H5

The cell addresses placed between [..] are absolute, the remaining cell addresses are relative and get a higher row/series address in each following line; e.g. in cell D6 we have ([D3]/[A3])*A6.

8 FURTHER READING

Little has been written on stunt kiting, for this type of kiting is still too young. Standard works like *Kites* by David Pelham and *Kites, an Historical Survey* by Clive Hart, only supply historical information. *Stuntkites!* by the American David Gomberg is a very interesting as well as amusing book which focuses on the art of stunt kiting; you will not find any construction plans in it. *Lenkdrachen, Bauen und Fliegen* by the German Wolfgang Schimmelpfennig, and *Lenkdrachen zum Nachbauen* by Thomas Erfurth and Harald Schlitzer do provide construction plans.

Then there is the *American Stunt Kite Quarterly,* a three-monthly magazine on stunt kiting, established in 1988 which tends to concentrate on the pilots, the men behind the grips, rather than on kites themselves.

The German magazine *Drachenmagazin* is more informative in this respect but focuses on Europe.

BOOKS

– Eden, Maxwell, *Kiteworks*, Sterling Publishing Co., Inc., New York, 1989.
– Erfurth, Thomas and Schlitzer, Harald, *Lenkdrachen zum Nachbauen*, Englisch Verlag, 1989.
– Gomberg, David, *Stuntkites!*, David Gomberg, Salem OR, 1988.
– Hart, Clive, *Kites, an Historical Survey*, Paul P. Appel, New York, 1982.
– Morgan, Paul and Helene, *The Book of Kites*, Dorling Kindersley Ltd., London, 1992.
– Moulton, Ron, *Kites*, Pelham Books, London, 1978.
– Pelham, David, *Kites*, Penguin Books Ltd., London, 1976.
– Schertel, Christine, *Skywork experience*, Skywork Agentur, Hamburg, 1991.
– Schimmelpfennig, Wolfgang, *Lenkdrachen, Bauen und Fliegen*, Falken Verlag, 1989.
– Yolen, Will, *The Complete Book of Kites and Kiteflying*, Simon and Schuster, New York, 1976.

MAGAZINES

– *American Kite*, Daniel Prentice, San Francisco.
– *Drachenmagazin*, Axel Voss Drachen Verlag, Hamburg, as from 1989.
– *Kitelines*, Aeolus Press, Baltimore.
– *Stunt Kite Quarterly*, Susan Batdorff, Manistee MI, as from 1988.
– *Vlieger*, Stichting Nederlandse Vliegerpromotie, The Hague (Holland), as from 1982.

9 CONVERSIONS

We strongly advize you to use as little conversion as possible. The kites in this book are based on the metric system; by converting measurements of the various plans into feet and inches you are likely to get 'odd' numbers. That is to say, converting the measurements, you will end up rounding off whereby precision will be lost. Why not buy yourself some metric rulers instead, it would be worth the investment.

LENGTH			**WEIGHT**			**SPEED**		
1 m	=	3.28 feet	1 kg	=	2.205 lb	1 km/h	=	0.62 mph
1 cm	=	0.394 inch	1 gram	=	0.035 oz			
1 mm	=	0.039 inch						

COMMON LINE BREAKING-STRENGTH

35 kg	–	80 lb	small kites/light wind kites
65 kg	–	150 lb	medium kites/team flying
90 kg	–	200 lb	large kites/strong wind team flying
135 kg	–	300 lb	power kites
225 kg	–	500 lb	traction kites

MOST OFTEN USED METRIC MATERIALS – IMPERIAL ALTERNATIVES

Ripstop nylon, 30 - 40 gram	–	0.75 oz
Solid fibreglass rod 3 - 4 mm	–	⅛″ glassfibre rod
Solid carbon fibre rod 2 - 3 mm	–	³⁄₃₂″ carbon rod, or ⅛″ glassfibre
Carbon fibre tube 6 mm	–	0.22 inches lighter alternative
	–	¼″ heavier alternative
Carbon fibre tube 8 mm	–	0.35 - 0.414 inch epoxy tube

WIND SPEED SCALE

Beaufort	m/s	km/h	mph	knots
1	0 - 2	0 - 7	0 - 4	0 - 4
2	2 - 3	7 - 11	4 - 7	4 - 6
3	3 - 5	11 - 20	7 - 13	6 - 11
4	5 - 8	20 - 28	13 - 18	11 - 16
5	8 - 11	28 - 38	18 - 24	16 - 21
6	11 - 14	38 - 50	24 - 31	21 - 28
7	14 - 17	50 - 61	31 - 38	28 - 34
8	17 - 20	61 - 72	38 - 45	34 - 40
9	20 - 24	72 - 86	45 - 54	40 - 48